VIROPHILIA

Cookbook in the 22nd Centu[ry]

病毒之愛

給二十二世紀
病毒愛好者的食譜書

VIROPHILIA

The 2070 revised edition
of the Postnatural Cookbook

病毒之愛

2070 年後自然再版病毒食譜書

P.Y.L.

Set Margins' #5

前言

《病毒之愛》是寫給二十二世紀人類，統整人類開拓日常生活中各種病毒正面用途的食譜書。

十七世紀雷文虎克（Leeuwenhoek）改進顯微鏡讓放大倍率足以放大細菌至肉眼可見尺度後，人類才確實理解細菌的物質性存在。

直至十九世紀微生物學開啟大門，科學家如費迪南德・柯恩（Ferdinand Cohn）、路易斯・巴斯德（Louis Pasteur）及羅伯特・柯赫（Robert Koch）因工具與研究方法的進步而開始對細菌有詳細的描述，並進一步改進微生物學的研究方式與工具。在此同時「衛生」概念與抗生素的使用首次進入人類認知，並在抗生素濫用後抗藥性的概念被建立。

二十世紀，人類意識到細菌與疾病的唯一並直接關聯是對於細菌的片面理解，並逐漸開始討論益生菌與生物菌叢。這個主流觀點的改變自微生物學開始發展兩百年後才出現。

而病毒的正式「發現」時間（也是病毒進入人類理解範圍的時刻）為二十世紀初期。此前，科學家與全人類認為病毒與細菌無異。

１９２０年始有科學家發現在細菌之外有種「可透過濾網的致病體（the filterable agents）」存在，並予以分離，病毒始正式進入人類視野。二十一世紀，病毒對其宿主的益處如植物病毒增加植物耐旱性、植物與昆蟲病毒能改變昆蟲行為等現象，正式被科學家納入研究範疇。

二十一世紀後期，人類對於病毒的觀點經歷劇烈轉變。哲學思維上開始重新思考人類作為生態系的一份子，刺激了人類從其他生物角度開始思考，並帶起探索病毒各種用途的研究。儘管在醫療領域中將病毒作為疫苗或基因療法的載體甚為古老，但二十一世紀當病毒的有益性研究經費相對稀缺的情況下，將病毒應用在食物與娛樂上是出乎意料且有趣的轉折。

本書寫作的主要目的在於呈現出人類與病毒在無偏見、無目的情況下建立精彩而非用途取向的互動關係之各種面向。

P.Y.L.

2068 年 6 月，阿姆斯特丹

Foreword

Virophilia is a cookbook written for the 22nd century human beings in consideration for incorporating the positive usage of viruses into our daily life.

It was in the 17th century, when Leeuwenhoek first invented the microscope with a resolution high enough to see bacteria that human beings had the first concrete knowledge of their physical existence.

In the 19th century, the door of microbiology opened when many scientists such as Ferdinand Cohn, Louis Pasteur, and Robert Koch started to describe bacteria in detail, and developed methods for handling them.

It was also at that time when we started to have the idea of 'hygiene' along with the discovery of antibiotics and antibiotic resistance.

Moving on to the 21st century, we have discovered the statement that 'bacteria are directly and only correlated with diseases' was problematic, hence the discussion around probiotics and microbiomes. Between the beginning of the study of microbiology and our current understanding of bacteria, there is a gap of approximately 200 years.

The 'discovery' of viruses, or more of how viruses finally enter the world we can observe, was at the beginning of the 20th century. Before that, scientists and the whole world considered viruses to be no different from bacteria.

It was only in the early 1920s that scientists were able to dissociate bacteria from 'the filterable agents' - a.k.a. viruses. And it was also then that we started to identify diseases that are caused by viruses. Scientists of the 21st century in different fields are starting to research the benefits that viruses could bring to their hosts, such as their abilities to help plants to endure drought or to change insects' behaviour.

The world has had a huge shift in perspective since the late 21st century. The world has returned to the consideration of human beings as a part of the whole ecosystem.

This also motivates human beings to view other biological beings in different ways, which leads to a series of explorations around different possible usage of viruses. Although the medical use of viruses such as vaccines and vectors for genetic therapy was not something unexpected, the movement of using viruses for food and pleasure is a rather different turn. As when it first appeared, the funding supporting non-medical research on viruses in the science field was comparatively scarce.

This cookbook is written to show the non-biased, intention-free relationship human beings can have with viruses which were not considered useful but are, in fact, fascinating.

P.Y.L.

June 2068, Amsterdam

Cotesia Congreta Bracovirus

A beneficial virus for wasps to suppress their host caterpillar's immune system in order to incubate wasp eggs.

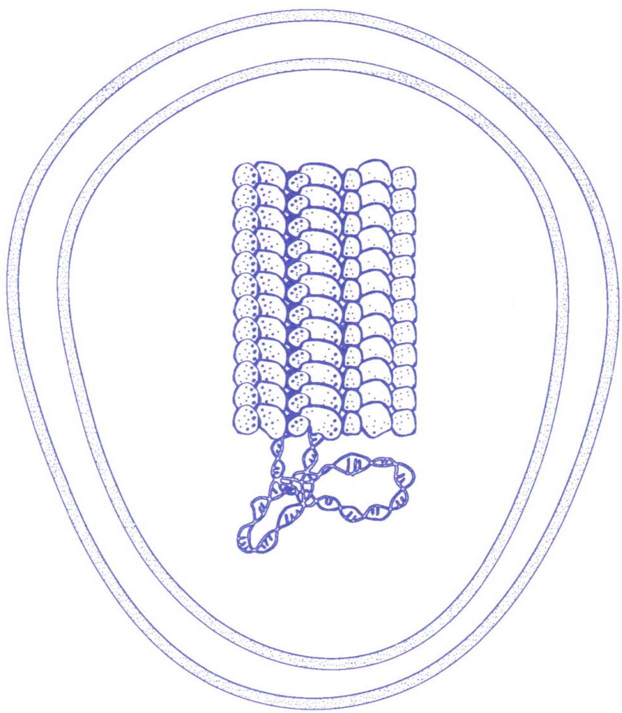

Chapter One

Simulating the Viral Experiences

病毒經驗模擬

ca. 2020

西元 2020 年前後

以非病毒食材模擬病毒食材在身體上作用，

以擴增人類對於病毒經驗的感官資料庫。

菜餚設計重點為觸發非持續性的生理與心理反應，

透過這過程從生理上理解病毒他者。

Simulation of viral ingredients with non-viral ingredients in order to expend our sensorial library towards viral agents.

Dishes can be designed to evoke non-prolonged physical and psychological reactions with human bodies. It is a gesture to understand the viral others at the physical level.

流感模擬

前菜

黏液噴霧

薑汁結蘭膠氣霧版，以吸入方式食用。

鮮薑搾汁。與結蘭膠、酒精混合，形成微黏的液體。將薑液裝入超音波霧化器中，霧化於空氣中。

主菜

火焰薑汁鴨湯

薑對半切。芝麻油炒薑。鴨肉切小塊後川燙。

以薑與酒燉鴨肉一小時。

以碗盛湯，加入１０毫升酒精並在上桌時點燃。

主菜

冰泡油炸辣椒球

將打發的 3% 海藻酸鈉於攝氏 0 度下冷藏成泡沫。

辣椒球以圓形糯米糰製成，以辣椒粉與辣椒油做餡。用菜籽油加熱至攝氏２３０度油炸。

甜點

薑辣蜜餞

薑切片。將１００毫升水加熱至沸騰，加入４００克糖至溶解。

糖溶解後，加入薑與辣椒。薑與辣椒在糖水中煮三分鐘，瀝乾並冷卻晾乾。

Influenza Sim.

Appetizer

Mucus Aerosol

This is gellan gum with ginger in the form of aerosol, eaten by breathing in.

Extract ginger juice from fresh ginger.

Mix with gellan gum and alcohol to create a slightly viscous liquid.

Load the ginger liquid into the ultrasonic fog generator and let the fog disperse in the surrounding space.

Main

Ginger Duck Soup in Flames

Cut the ginger in half.

Fry the ginger with sesame oil.

Cut the duck into pieces. Blanch the duck.

Stew the duck with ginger and rice alcohol for 1 hour.

The soup is served in bowls. Add 10ml of alcohol and light it on fire (on the table) when serving.

Main

Deep Fried Chilli Dumpling in Icy Foam

The foam is made with whipped 3% sodium alginate milk solution at 0°C.

The chilli dumplings are made of round, glutenous rice dough with cayenne pepper flakes and oil filling.

Deep Fry at 230°C using canola oil.

Dessert

Candied Ginger and Chili

Slice the ginger.

Heat up 100 ml of water until it boils.

Add 400g of sugar.

When the sugar is fully dissolved, add the ginger and chilli.

Cook the ginger and chilli for 3 mins. Drain the liquid, and leave the ginger and chilli to cool and dry.

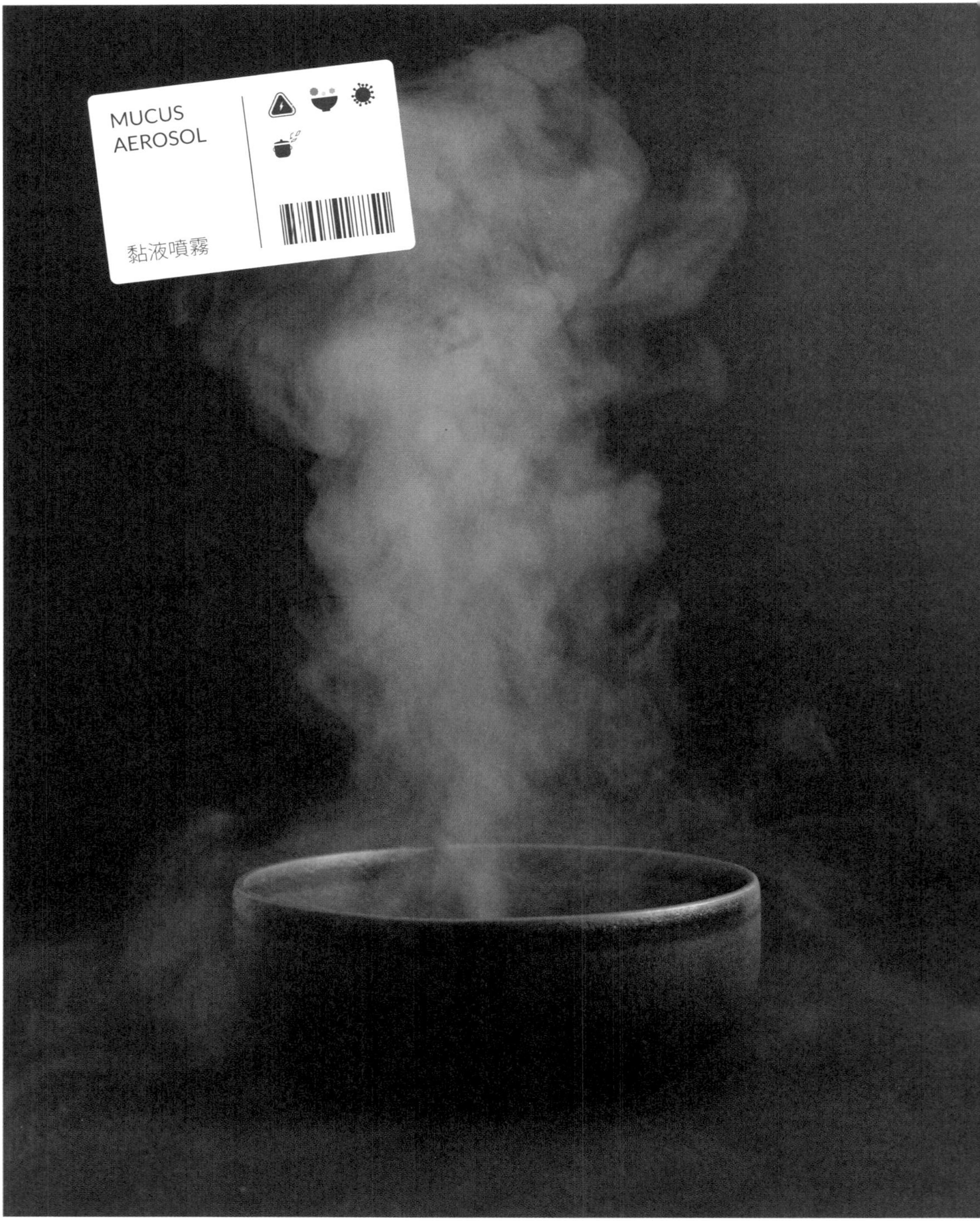
MUCUS
AEROSOL
黏液噴霧

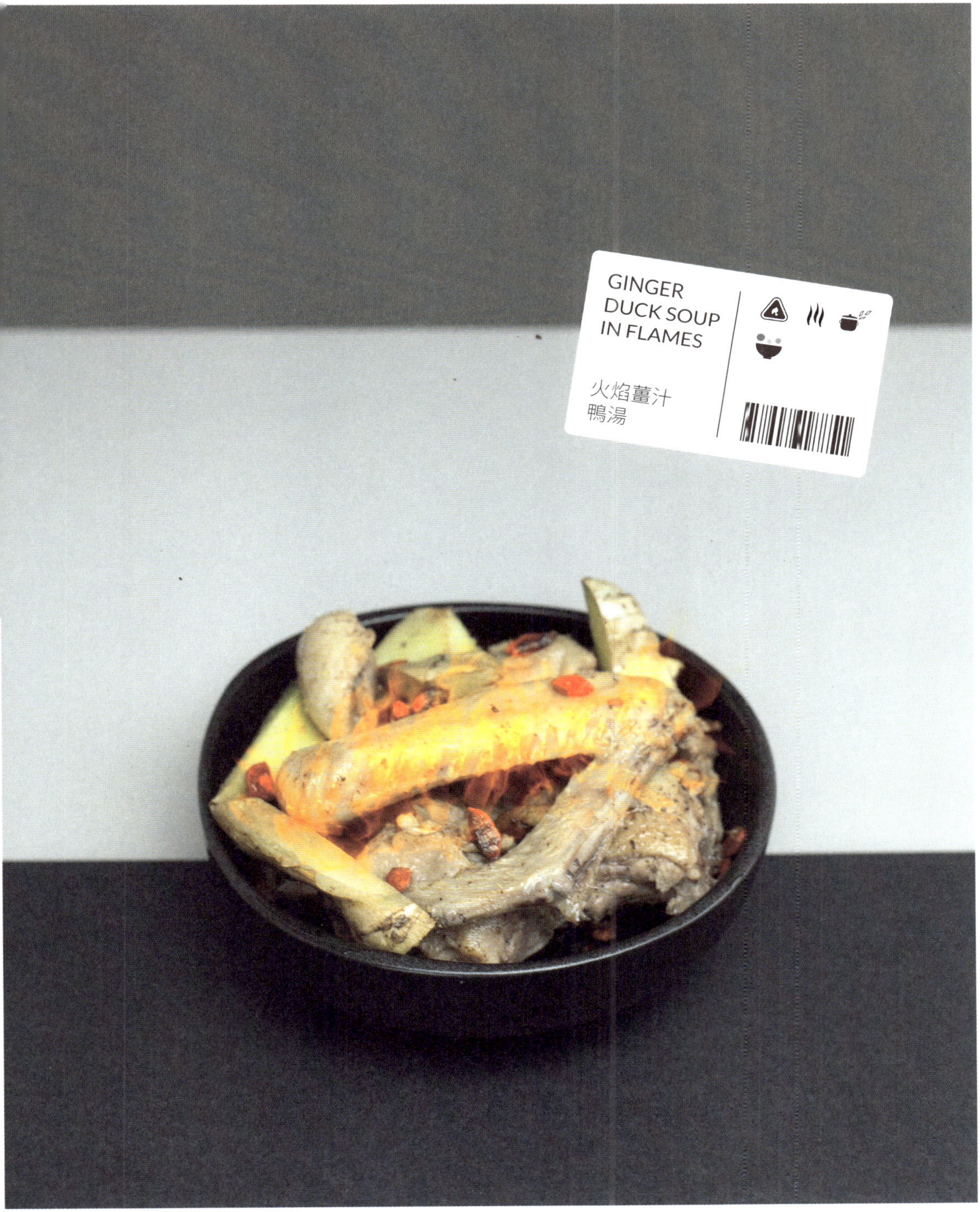
GINGER
DUCK SOUP
IN FLAMES
火焰薑汁
鴨湯

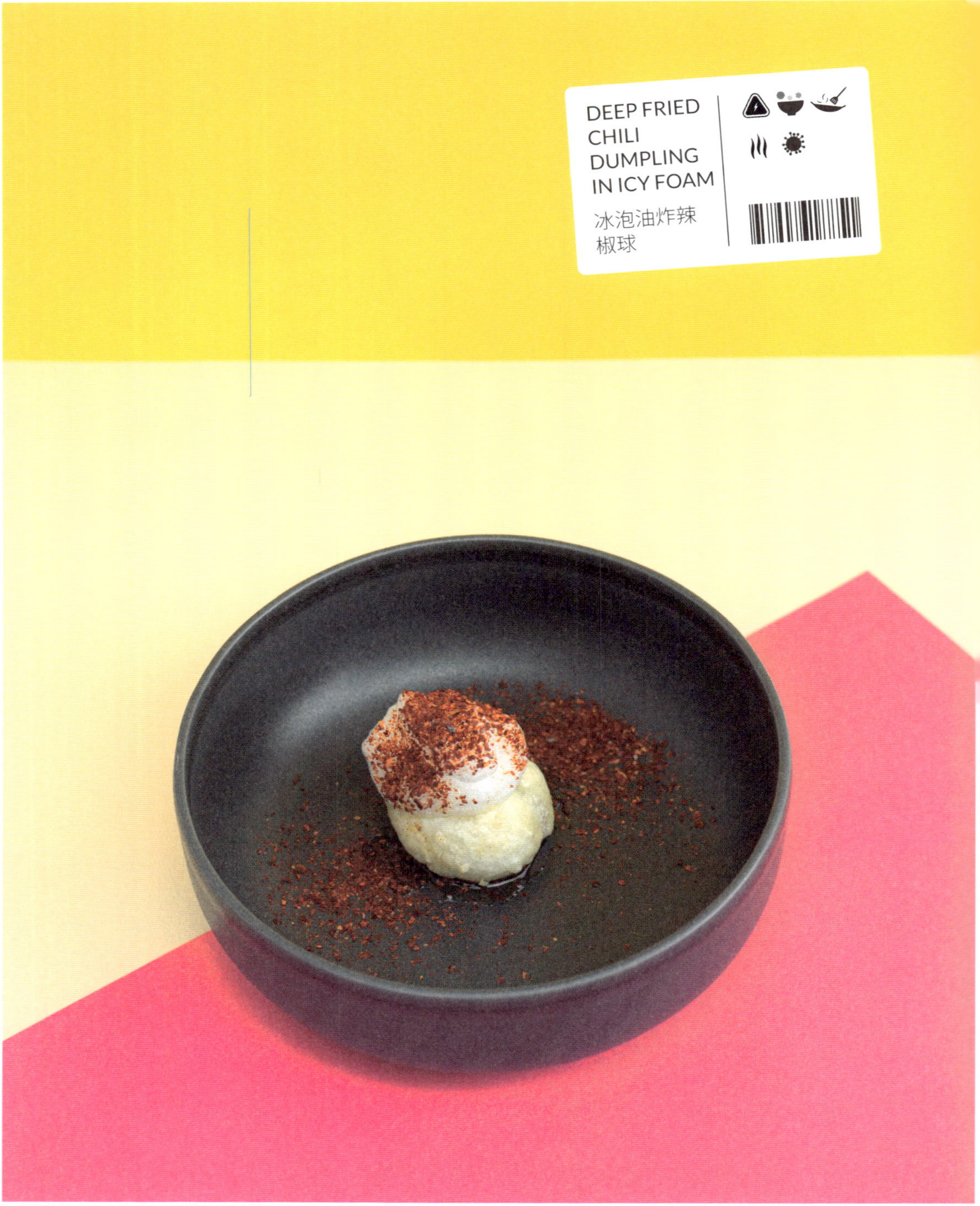
DEEP FRIED
CHILI
DUMPLING
IN ICY FOAM
冰泡油炸辣
椒球

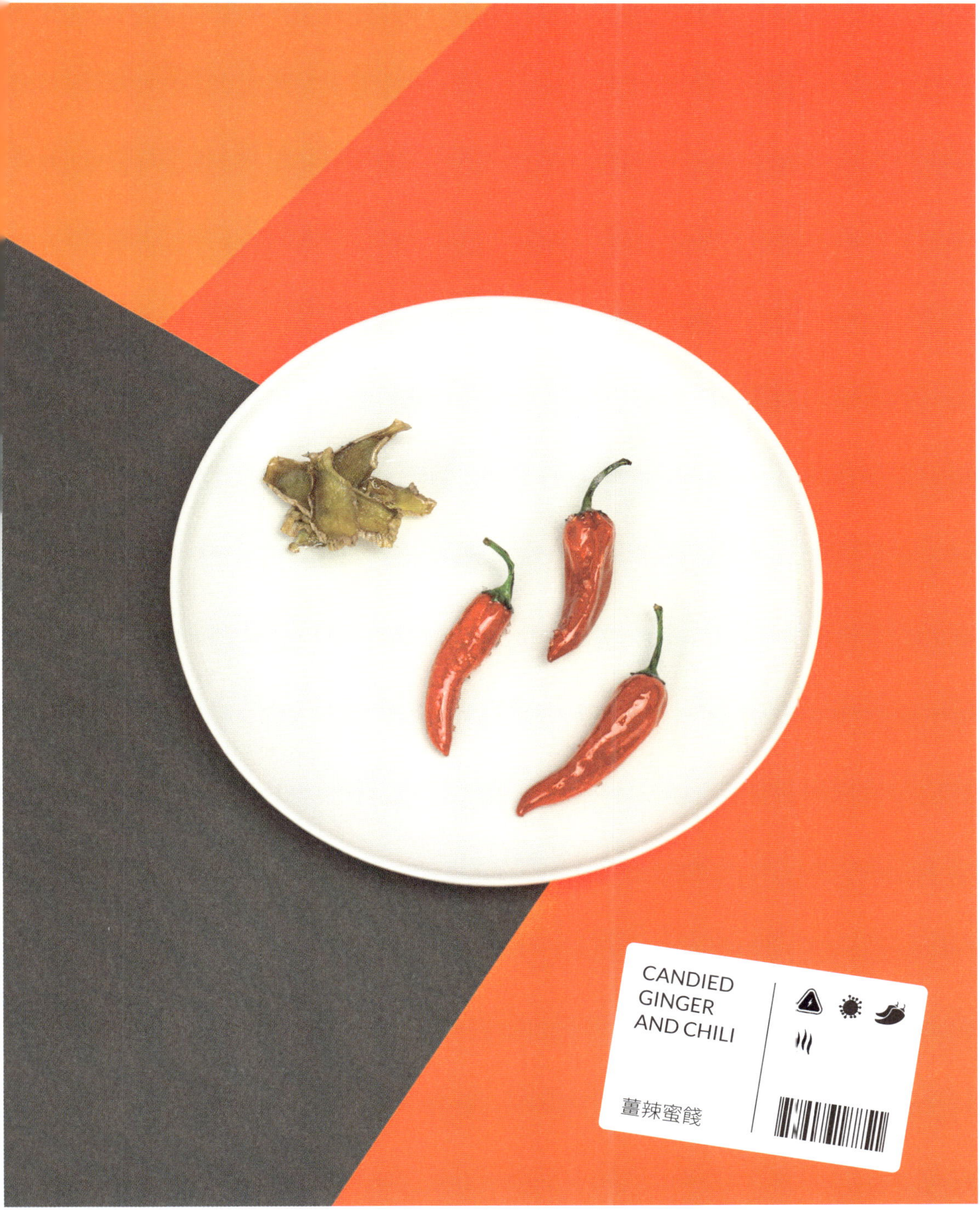
CANDIED
GINGER
AND CHILI
薑辣蜜餞

諾羅病毒模擬

前菜

狂風暴雨前的生蠔

吐根醬西瓜塊辣椒油與芝麻油魚子佐生蠔

備好 1% 海藻酸鈉溶液與 0.5% 乳酸鈣溶液。將一杯辣油與海藻酸鈉溶液混合。用針筒將容液滴入 0.5% 乳酸鈣溶液中。在滴入的液體表面會形成一層薄膜，變成類似魚子醬的顆粒。

將一杯麻油與海藻酸鈉溶液混合。重複前一步驟，製作麻油魚子。西瓜切丁。將生蠔打開置於盤中，放上辣油與麻油魚子、西瓜丁。淋上 1/8 茶匙的吐根醬。

沙拉

蓖麻油拌鬆脆葉綠蔬菜

將結球萵苣、蓮藕與白蘿蔔洗淨後切碎混合。

淋上蓖麻油。

主菜

腹部電擊鮪魚生魚片

將鮪魚生魚片用利刃精巧裁切爲 1 0cm x 5 cm 的長型方塊。上菜時也同時端上電療機一台。將電療機的電極分別皆在肚臍上方與下方。

當生魚片被刀子切割時，電療機便送出電脈衝刺激腹部收縮並觸發疼痛。

甜點

覆盆子雪酪

用果汁機將水、糖、覆盆子攪打至混合並冷凍一晚。

將隔夜的冷凍果泥放進冰淇淋機中攪拌 1 0 分鐘，直接食用。

Norwalk Sim.

Appetizer

Oyster before Storm

Chilli Oil and Sesame Oil Caviar Oyster with Ipecac Sauce and Watermelon Chops.

Prepare 1% sodium alginate solution and 0.5% sodium lactate solution.

Mix 1 cup of chilli oil with sodium alginate.

Use a syringe to make drops of the solution into 0.5% sodium lactate solution. A thin layer of film will form around the droplet, creating caviar-like bubbles.

Mix 1 cup of sesame oil with sodium alginate. Repeat the same steps above to make the sesame oil caviar.

Chop the watermelon into small square pieces.

Prepare fresh oysters on the plate, and dress the oysters with chili oil caviar, sesame oil caviar and watermelon chops.

Pour 1/8 teaspoon of Ipecac sauce on top of each oyster.

Salad

Crunchy Leafy Greens Dressed with Caster Oil

Wash iceberg lettuces, lotus roots, and white radishes thoroughly.

Chop the lettuces, lotus roots and white radishes.

Mix together.

Dress the salad with caster oil.

Main

Tuna Sashimi with Electrical Stimulation on Abdomen

Fresh tuna meat is served in pieces of 10cm x 5cm with a very sharp knife. An electrical massage machine is served along with the dish. Put one of the massage machine electrodes right above the belly button and the other right below. Massage machine sends out electrical pulses whenever the tuna is being cut by the knife.

Dessert

Raspberry Sorbet

Use a blender to blend water, sugar and raspberries together.

Freeze overnight.

Put the juice into the ice-cream machine for 10 mins.

Serve cold.

Note

Chilli and sesame induce low fever. Ipecac induces vomiting. Caster oil induces diarrhoea. Electrical stimulation on abdomen triggers abdomen muscle contractions. Sorbet increases intestine discomfort.

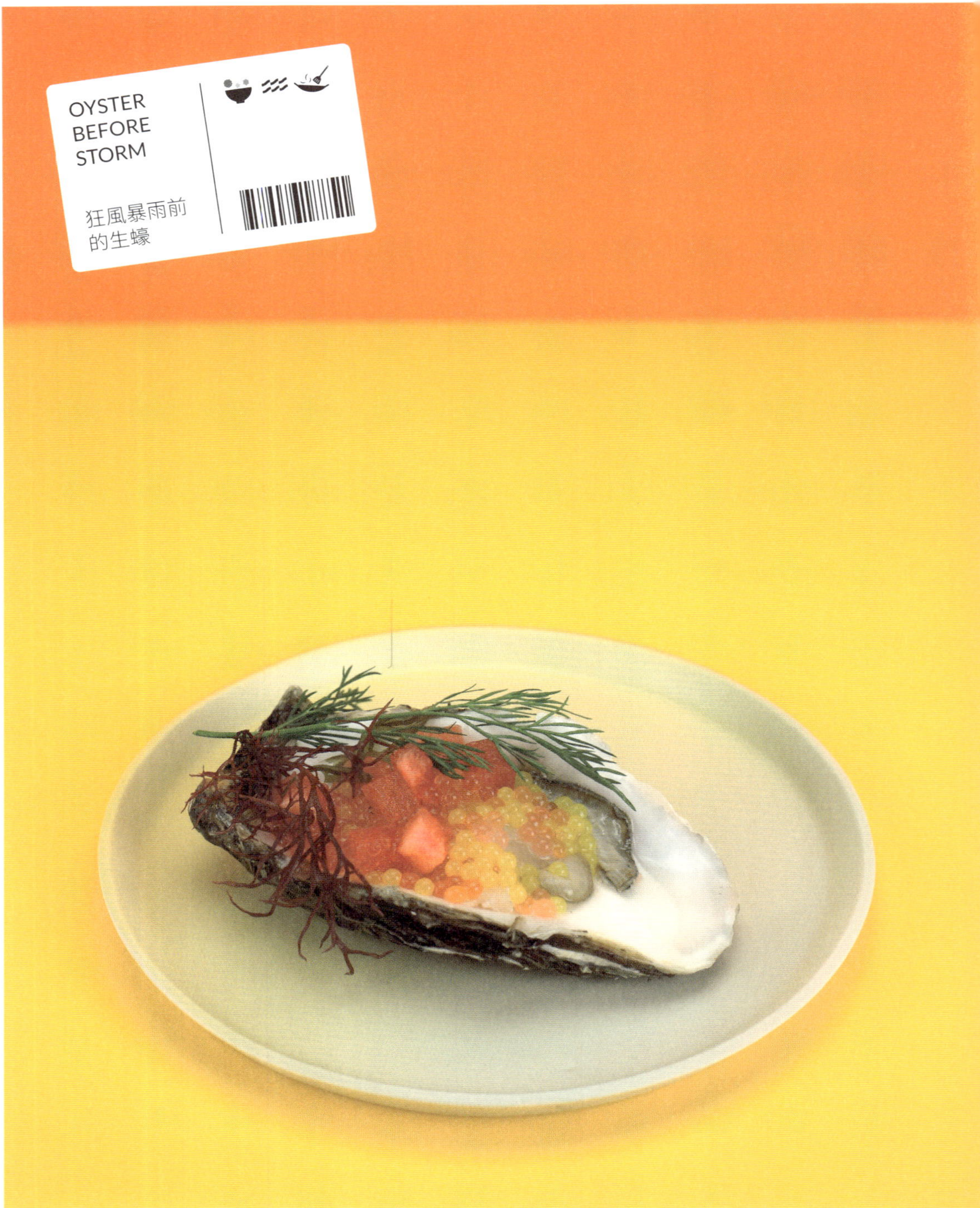
OYSTER
BEFORE
STORM
狂風暴雨前
的生蠔

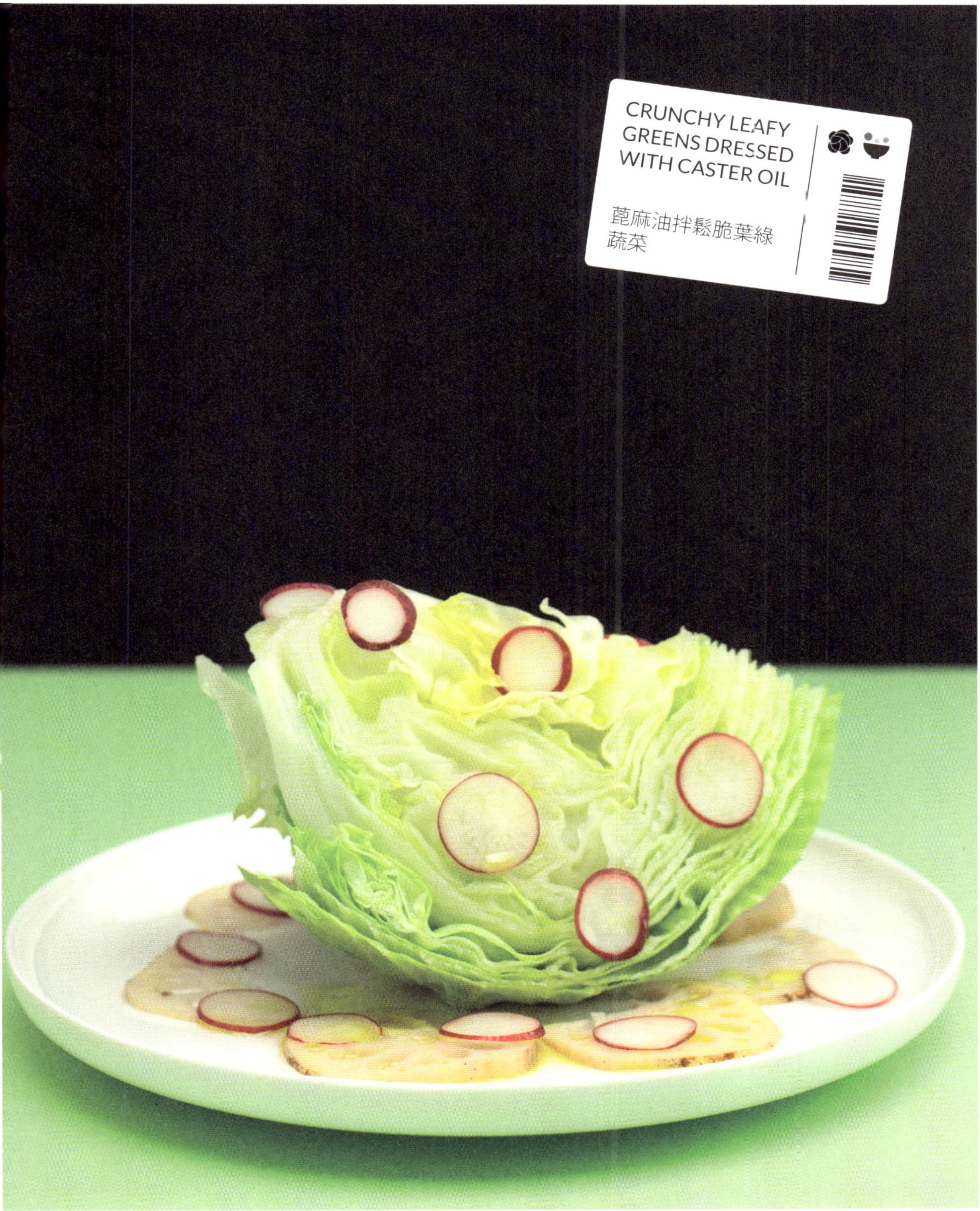
CRUNCHY LEAFY
GREENS DRESSED
WITH CASTER OIL
蓖麻油拌鬆脆葉綠
蔬菜

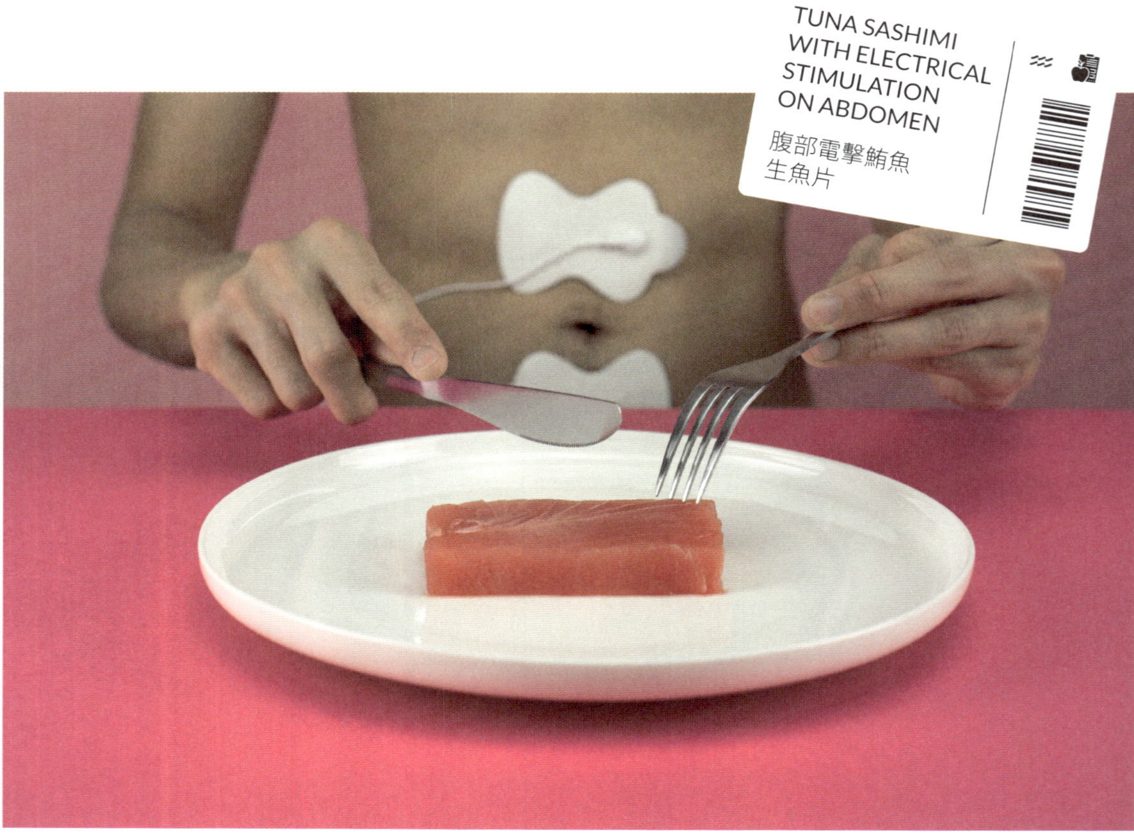
TUNA SASHIMI
WITH ELECTRICAL
STIMULATION
ON ABDOMEN
腹部電擊鮪魚
生魚片

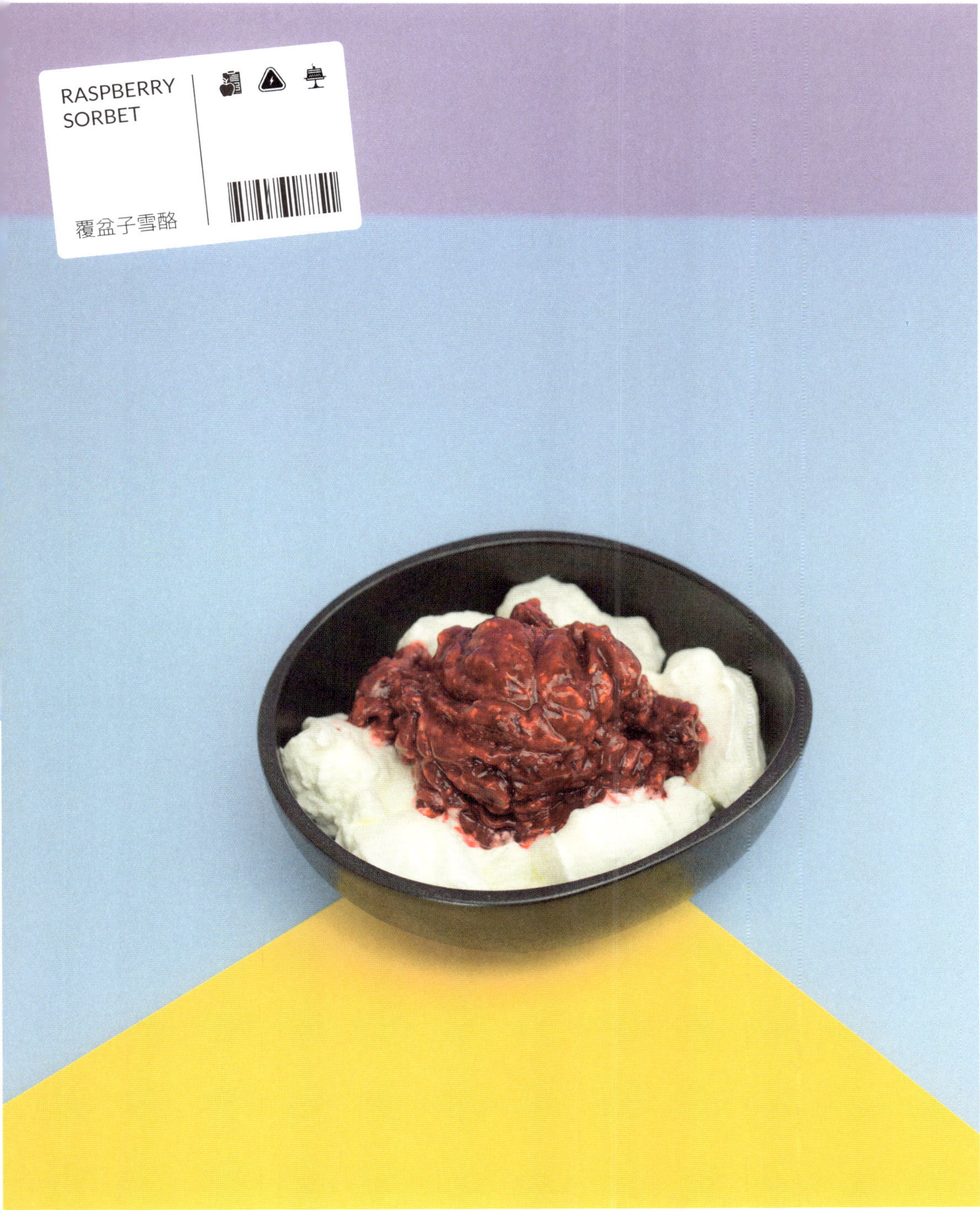
RASPBERRY
SORBET
覆盆子雪酪

Pea Enation Mosaic Virus

Actually two viruses that cannot live without each other.

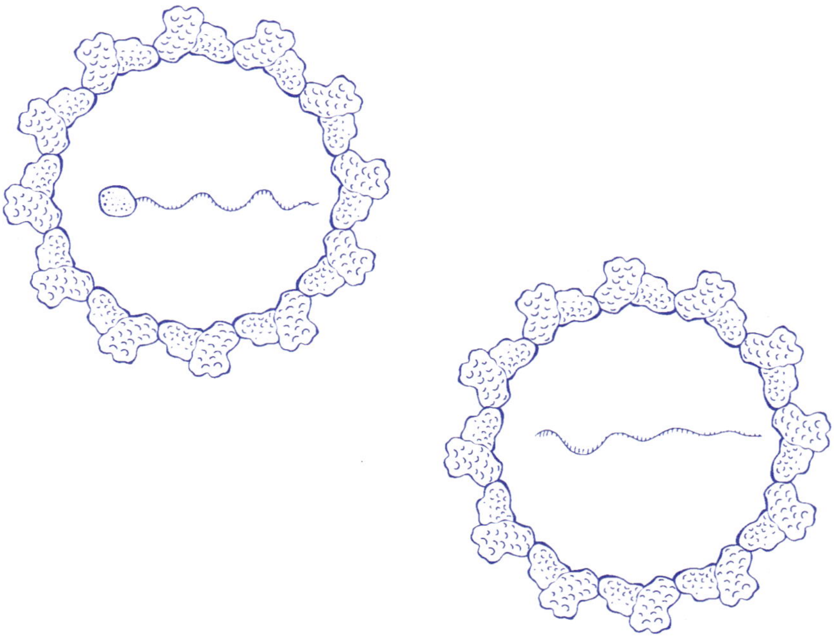

Chapter Two

Viral Fermentation

病毒發酵

ca. 2037

西元 2037 年前後

發酵不僅在細胞生物中發生，也在其他類生物體上發生。

病毒可以是益生病毒的角色，也可以扮演發酵中的關鍵。

需要精確的病毒控制能力。

病毒－宿主互動可以讓食材產生質感、味道與形態上的優勢。

Fermentation does not exclusively take place in cellular organisms but also other semi-living beings. Viruses can be used either as probiotics or as the key role in fermentation.

Precise control on virus strains is needed. Virus-Host interactions provide advantages to either the texture, taste, or morphologies of the ingredients.

諾羅發酵

諾羅發酵使用諾羅病毒在活生物體內發酵。諾羅病毒透過感染，改變動物的腸道結構（在此我們不使用「生病」一詞，因感染是人爲且刻意的）。腸道因爲感染而變得較爲平滑，失去平常讓腸道表面粗糙的腸道絨毛。儘管正常小腸以其爽脆口感受人稱道，腸道絨毛所造成的粗糙感有些時候不受歡迎。平滑的腸道紋理更細膩，深受專業美食家喜愛。

養殖方式

羅發酵農場必須隨時關注諾羅病毒的存活狀態，以確保農場裡的諾羅病毒持續生長。

動物身體透過感染獲得免疫力，而在這過程中諾羅病毒會經歷複製、感染、消滅的階段。因此，飼主必須在前一隻病毒發酵中的動物將體內病毒消滅以前，將病毒接種到「乾淨的」新動物身上。體內正有諾羅病毒複製中的動物通常是最適合收成的時候，因爲腸道平滑的症狀最容易在這個時刻發生。

農場必須隨時準備足夠的動物來連續接種。由於諾羅病毒的特性，每一批接種動物需要接種後四天出貨。因此，會根據市場需求，農場決定該批接種要接種幾隻。如果拖延太久才接種下一批，則飼主可能失去現有的病毒株。

監測病毒的突變與微突變也非常重要。因此，飼主會密切觀察動物們的健康狀態。如果出現重症，則立刻將該動物隔離，並消毒整個農場，以防突變的病毒株散佈。

同時，確保動物不會因爲病毒的感染而死亡也極爲重要。當動物死亡的那刻開始，其肉體便開始腐爛而不適合食用，確保肉的品質則最好在動物活著時屠宰。

飼主們傾向於培養溫和的病毒株，以確保動物能維持感染狀態夠久到把體內廢物都吐出、排洩出來。這個農場病毒株也擅長於讓腸道結構改變並且較流行的病毒株來得不容易傳播，以便農場操作與使用。

有些人也認爲經過諾羅病毒感染發酵的動物比較「潔淨」，因爲動物在被屠宰之前已「自我潔淨」過了。

Noro-Fermentation

Noro-fermentation uses Norovirus as an in-body fermentation on animals while alive. The infection of norovirus changes the morphology of the intestine of infected animals. (Here we do not say 'sick,' since it is intentional). The intestine becomes more smooth, losing its intestinal villi. Although normal intestines are famous for their crunchiness, sometimes the villi can result in rough surfaces, which are not always preferable. The smoothened intestine has a much more delicate texture that is loved by many people.

Farming Metods

Noro-fermentation farms always keep a good eye on the survival of Norovirus so that they will never run out of Norovirus. Animal bodies gain immunity through infection.

During the process Norovirus will go through the cycle of replication, infection, and elimination. The farmers must transfer / inoculate a new 'clean' animal before the previous animal eradicates all the virus from its body. An animal with replicating Norovirus is usually at its best stage for harvesting, because it is most likely to have the desired symptoms, such as smoothened intestines.

The farms will keep enough numbers of animals for serial inoculation. Each 'unit' takes 4 days, and depending on market demand, the farmer decides how many animals each unit will contain. However, each unit must be harvested / slaughtered every 4 days due to the cycle of Norovirus. If waiting for longer, the farmer will risk losing his current Norovirus strain. Monitoring the mutation / micro-mutation of the virus is also important. Therefore, the farmers will closely observe the well-being of the animals. If severe symptoms appear, the animal will enter quarantine immediately, and the whole farm will be sanitised immediately so the mutated strain won't spread out of control. It is also crucial for the farmers that the animals do not die due to infection. As soon as the animal dies, the meat starts to rot. It is better if the animals are slaughtered.

The farmers tend to grow Norovirus strains that keep the animal infected for longer but milder just enough for the animal to puke / shit out everything in the body. The specific strain is also selected for its ability to cause optimal morphological change of the animal's intestine while keeping it less contagious than the epidemic strains for ease of handling within the farm.

Some people also prefer Norovirus-infected animals since they are more 'clean,' in the sense that the animals 'self-cleansed' themselves before being slaughtered.

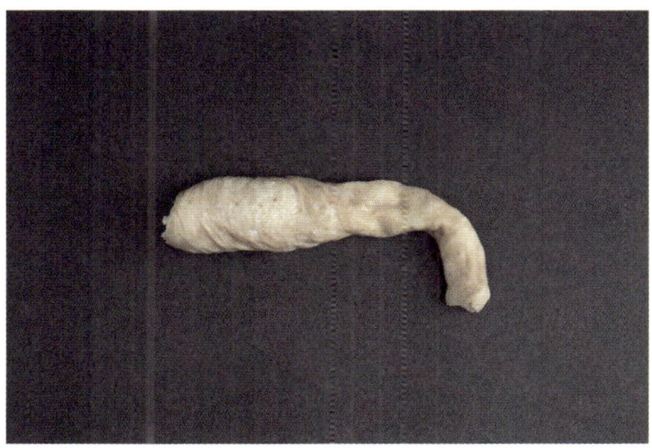

發酵後較爲平滑的豬大腸

Fermented pig intestine displaying a smoother surface and texture

乾旱釀造法

人類已知道有許多病毒能讓植物更耐旱。這個知識曾顛覆了植物栽培文化——讓人們從提供植物最理想的且無壓力的生長環境，變成提供植物有點壓力但不至於致死的生長環境，來增加果實的甜度

這個現象通常發生在特別建造密集栽培的農場中。剛進貨的植物是「乾淨」的植物，也就是沒有感染到農場中病毒的植物。農夫們會將需要的病毒用海綿擦在植物上來接種。所有農夫在溫室中作業時必須全身穿著防護衣，並且溫室有雙層門控管以防止任何生物在未控管的情況下進入。

病毒在植物上生活的過程中，植物也在逐漸地適應病毒的存在。感染了病毒的植物葉子開始出現不同顏色與花紋。農夫在見到病毒的存在後，可以開始減少給水量，讓植物用較少的水生長。雖然這樣會讓植物生長的速度與果實的產量變慢變低，但水量的減少也讓果實中的糖含量增加。

這樣意想不到的甜度讓水果多了一層有趣的味道。有些人說與香瓜茄嵌紋病毒共同生長的番茄吃以來就像是番茄蜜餞一般，乾燥後表皮上帶著一層薄薄的糖分，就像亞洲的柿餅一樣。同樣的耕作方法也被應用在橘子、漿果與甜椒上。

Pruning in the Drought

Throughout the years, it has been widely known that some viruses make plants more resistant to drought. This knowledge has changed the whole plant growing culture: from giving plants the most ideal, stress free environment, towards an environment that's stressful enough (but not enough for them to die) to reach a higher sweetness of fruit bearing.

This phenomenon usually happens within a purposefully built, densely packed farm. The new plants coming in are 'clean' plants, meaning free from the viruses grown in the farm. Farmers will rub the desired viruses on the leaves of the plants using a sponge to inoculate the plants. All the farmers entering the greenhouses will be dressed in hazmat suits. The greenhouses are controlled with double doors to prevent uncontrolled entries.

The viruses will be living on the plants as the plants accommodate to them. The foliages will start to appear in different colours and patterns. With the viruses' presence, the farmers are able to give much less water to the plants and allow the plants to grow with less water. Although this slows down the growing speed and yielding of the fruit, the dryness makes the sugar content higher in the fruits.

Such unexpected sweetness of fruit creates fascinating tastes. Some people describe the tomatoes grown with a selective Pepino Mosaic Virus as 'almost like tomato candite' on the skin of which sugar crystals literally form when they are dried, just like how Asian people dry persimmon. Other plants produced with the same farming method include oranges, berries, and peppers.

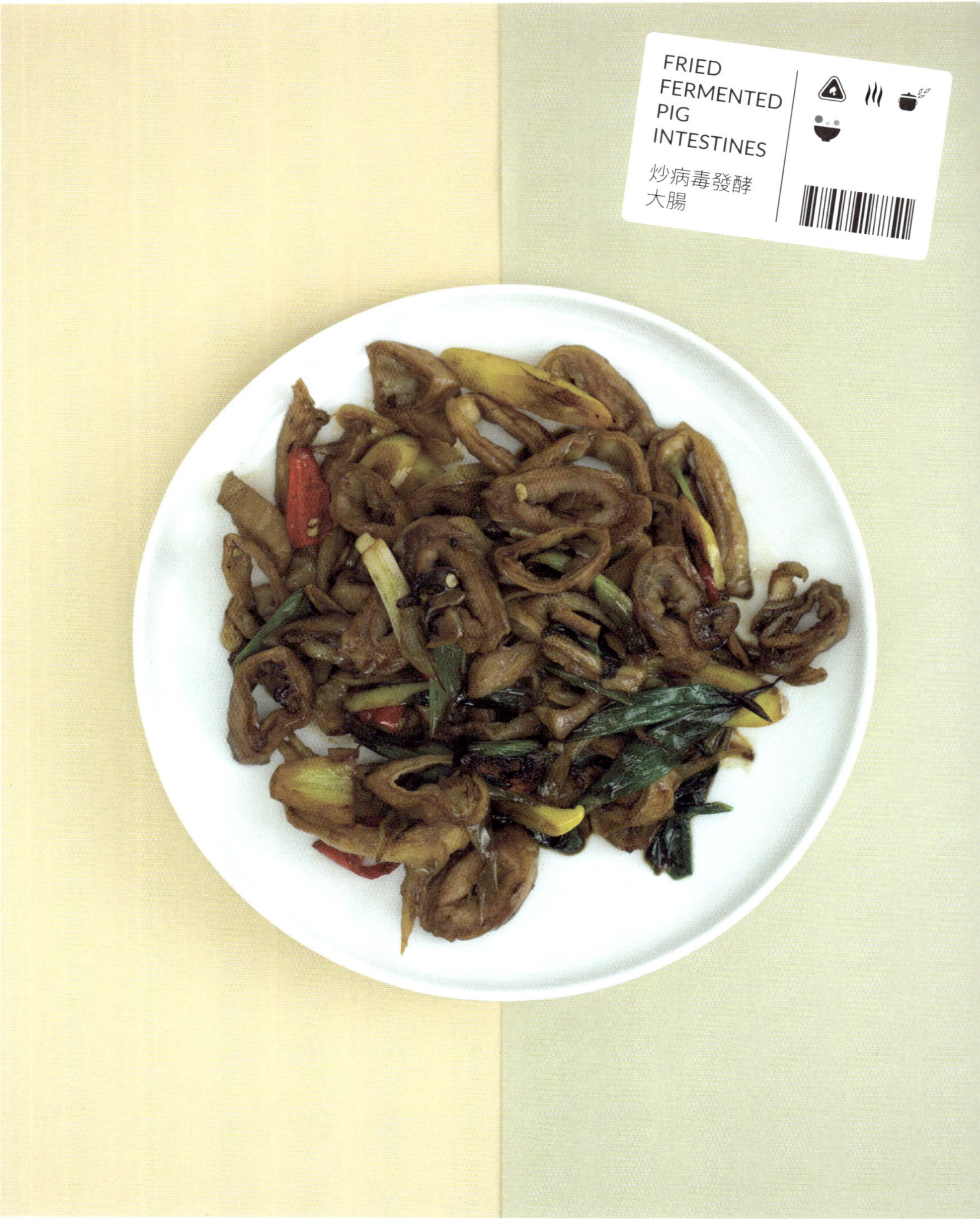
FRIED
FERMENTED
PIG
INTESTINES
炒病毒發酵
大腸

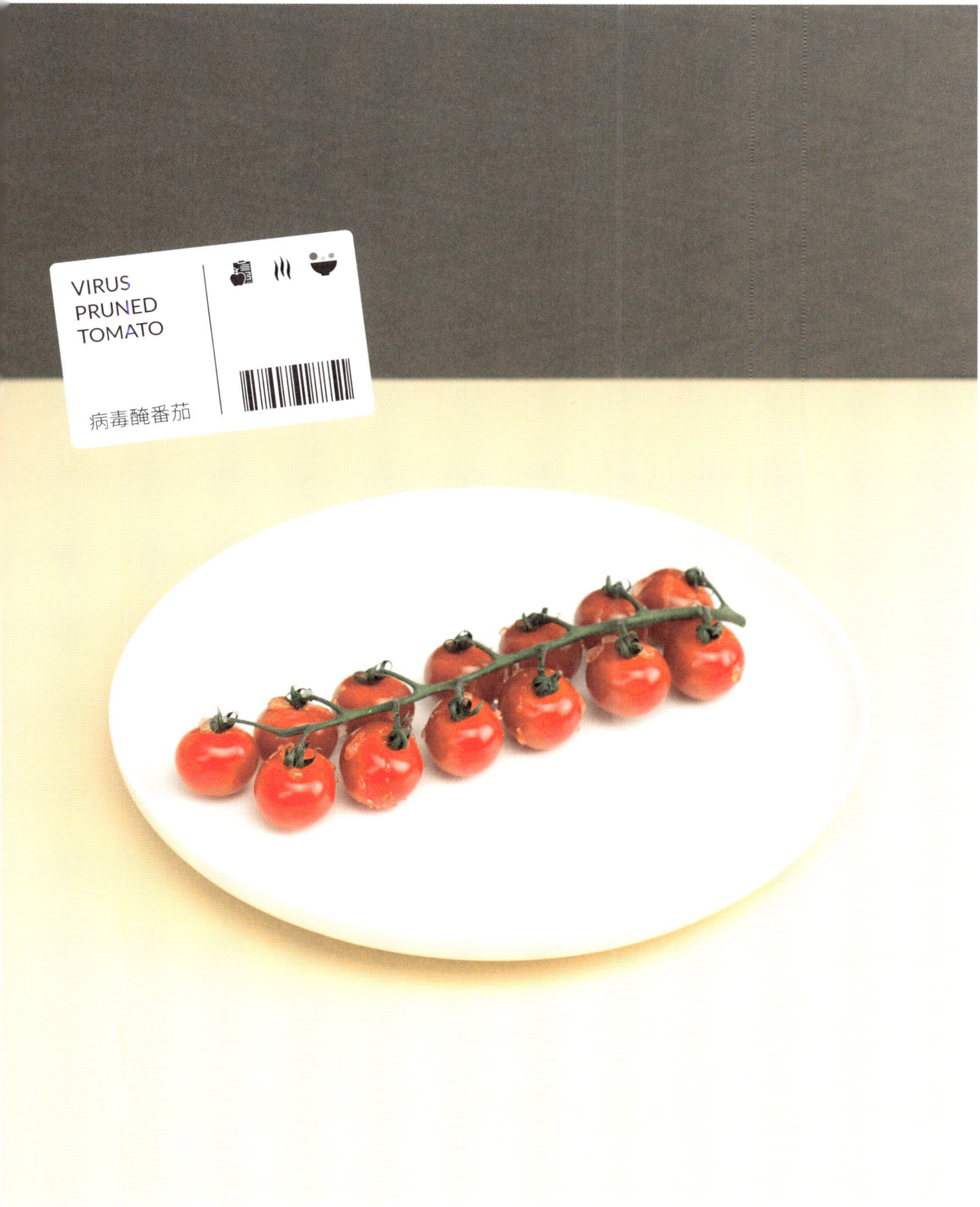
VIRUS
PRUNED
TOMATO
病毒腌番茄

Ebola Virus

A deadly virus that infects humans and primates, killed over 11,000 people during the outbreak in West Africa between 2013-2015.

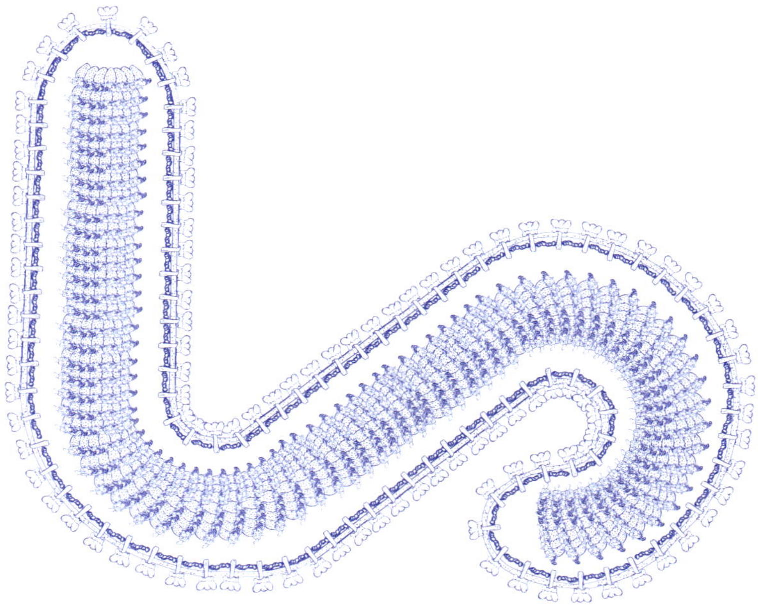

Chapter Three

Viruses as Active Ingredients

病毒做為有效成分

ca. 2042

西元 2042 年前後

食物中的有效成分不只包含化學分子也包含生物結構。

因此，思考食物與身體上的生物互動是重要的。

病毒可被當作益生病毒、疫苗或香料使用。

需要特別著重病毒與宿主互之間所創造的擴增身體經驗。菜色可以不僅是食物而是活的食物。

Active ingredients in food include not only chemical molecules, but also active biological components.

It is crucial to consider the biological interaction between the 'food' and the physical body.

Viruses can be used as probiotics, vaccines, or spices. Emphasis on the extended bodily experiences through virus-host interaction is needed. Cuisines can be not only 'food-food' but living food.

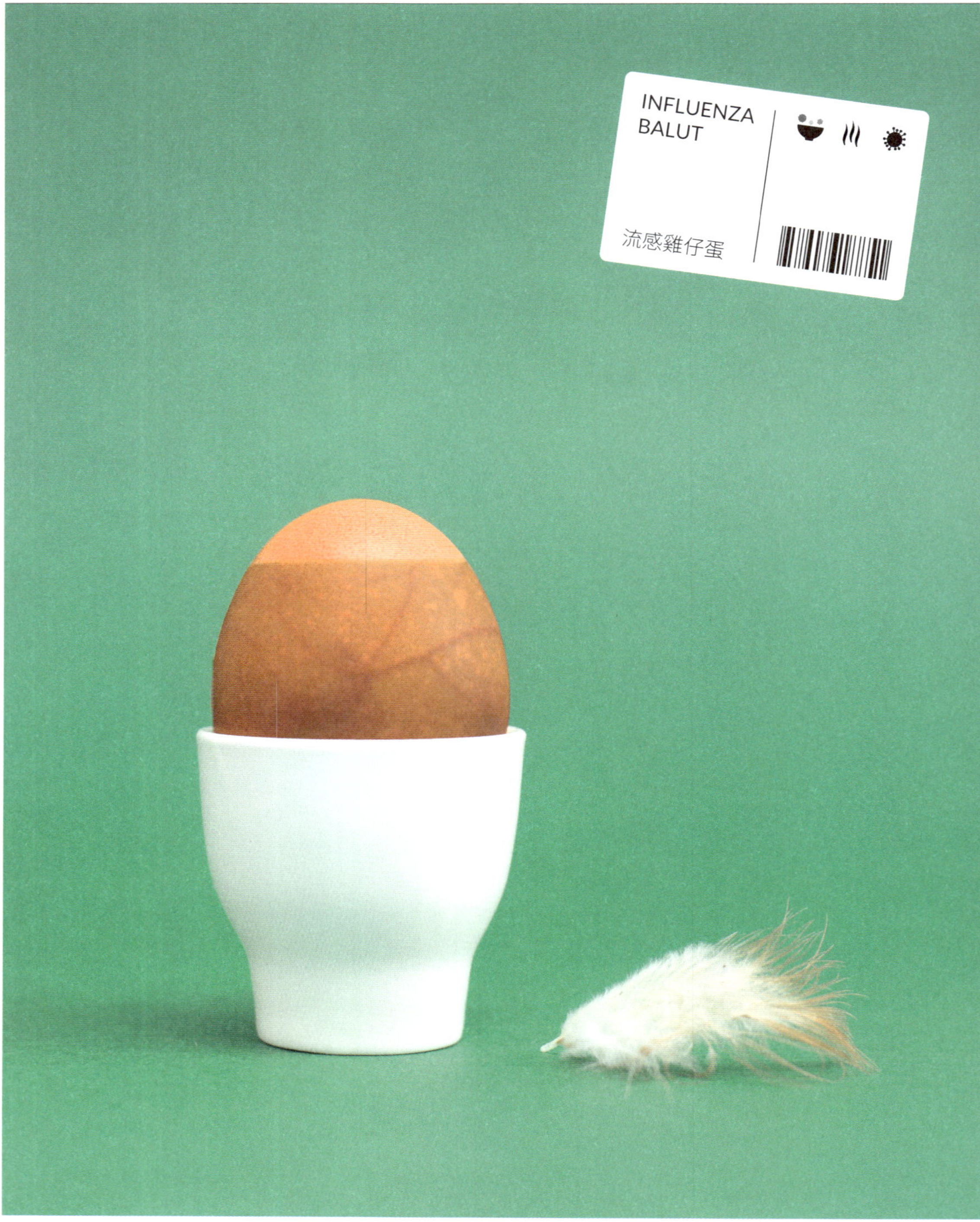
INFLUENZA
BALUT
流感雞仔蛋

流感雞仔蛋

流感病毒具有誘發高燒、喉嚨疼痛、咳嗽、肚子痛，以及頭暈與幻覺的能力。在身體反應如體溫上升、畏寒、發抖、以及高燒到一定體溫後產生的幻覺。烹飪用流感病毒株是經由特別培育篩選後得到的弱病毒株，也是流感病毒疫苗研發過程中的副產品。與醫用流感病毒旨在不引起生理不適，烹飪用流感病毒株會在人體上產生短暫輕微的生理不適，而這也是它的賣點。

市面上有許多不同的烹飪用病毒株，但對於每個人，由於免疫系統的記憶，每種病毒株只會在身體上「活躍」一次。儘管有些麻疹病毒株可以將免疫記憶清除，但不被建議太常使用以免其他有用的免疫記憶也被消除。這個食譜有些時候也會讓害怕打針的人們用來作爲不用打針的流感疫苗接種。與著名的南亞菜餚鴨仔蛋類似，大量生產的流感雞蛋爲介於10-11天的受精卵，此時雞胚胎已成形。在陰暗的房間裡，將光線照進雞蛋裡，可以看到雞蛋的氣室發亮。將房間的燈打開，並把雞蛋氣室那端朝上放置。小心地將氣室那側的殼用湯匙打開，接著會看到一層薄膜。薄膜戳開一個小孔，把蛋白倒出收集。 將蛋放在蛋架上，中火蒸10分鐘。打開蛋，半成形的雞胚胎躍然眼前。放涼。將胚胎與蛋白混合，用鹽調味，即可食用。 這道菜鮮味多汁，並在接下來四天內出現些微發熱狀態。因此，此道菜通常會配合超過四天的用餐體驗設計。

Influenza Balut

Influenza viruses are naturally capable of inducing/causing high fever, sore throat, coughing, abdominal pain, and potentially drowsiness, alongside hallucinations. Physical reactions include higher body temperatures, chills, shivering, and potentially hallucinations when the fever has reached a certain temperature. A suitable influenza virus strain for culinary use has been selectively 'bred' from the more virulent strains and was a byproduct of influenza vaccines: unlike the vaccines in medicine that aim to bring no physical reactions, the culinary influenza still triggers temperate physical reactions in the human body.

There are many different culinary strains available on the market. However, for each person, each strain is 'active' only once in a lifetime, due to the effect of the immune system. Although there are some measles products that wipe out your immune memories, it is not recommended to use them too often, because of the side effects of wiping out other useful immunity memories.

Sometimes this recipe is used for those who are afraid of needles and need seasonal flu (influenza) protection as well. Similar to the infamous South Asian dish Balut, industrial influenza chicken eggs are 10-11 days old fertilised chicken eggs in which the chicken embryo has already formed. In a comparatively dark room, shine the light through the egg. You can see the air cell light up. Turn on the light, put the air cell side up. Carefully open the shell on the air cell side with a spoon.

Now you can see the membrane. Open a small hole in the membrane, pour and collect the egg whites. Put the egg onto an egg stand. Steam the egg for 10 mins. Open the egg, and you will now see the cooked, half-formed chicken embryo. Leave it to chill. Mix the embryo with the egg whites. Season with salt. Ready to eat.The dish shall taste juicy and slightly gamy, with a follow-up of feverish symptoms which occur within 4 days. Therefore, this dish is usually combined with a dining experience which lastts more than 4 days.

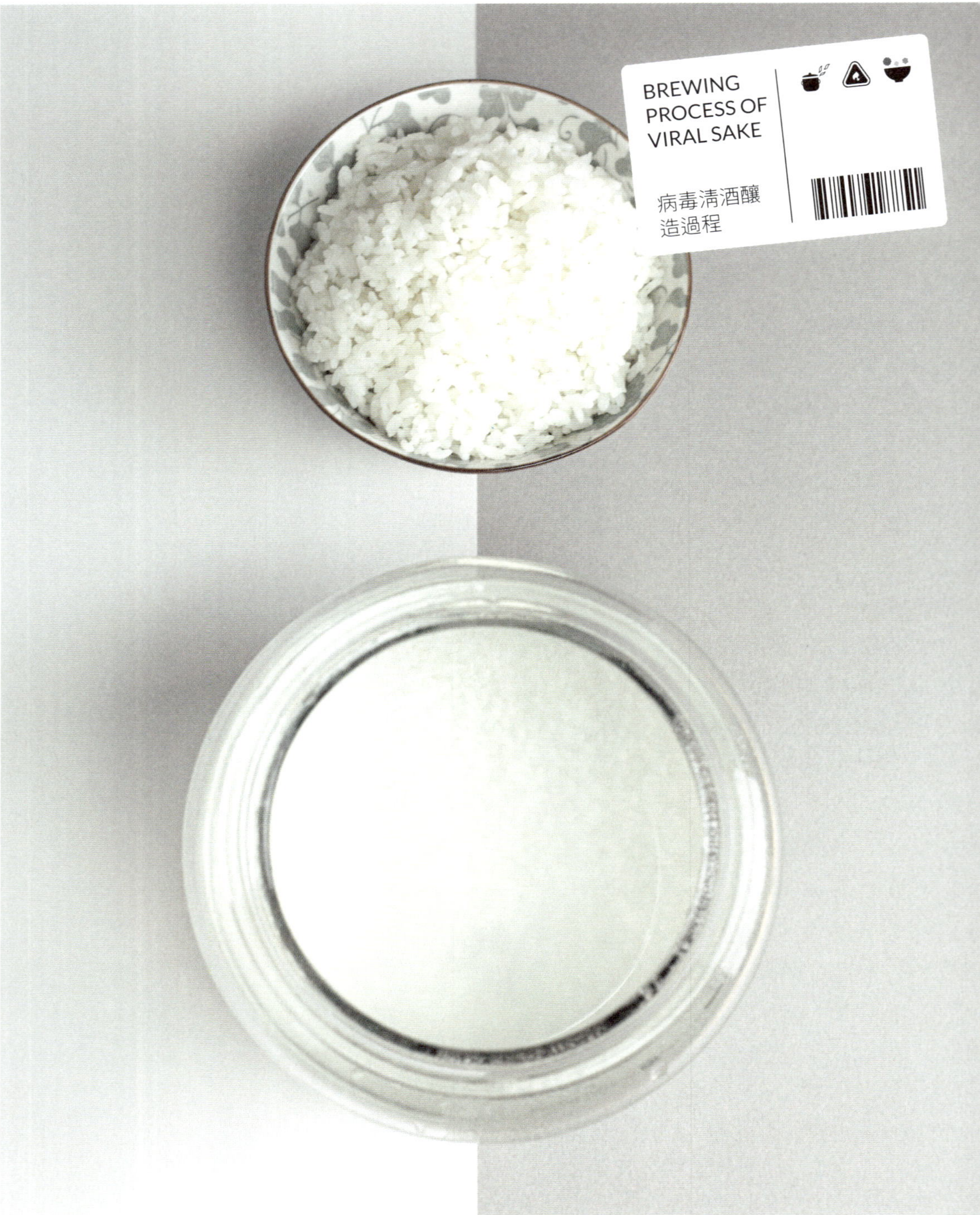
BREWING
PROCESS OF
VIRAL SAKE
病毒清酒釀
造過程

SM釀酒法

此爲史上第一款使用病毒釀製而成的飲料——雖然完全不符合傳統對於飲料的定義。這是個食譜，也是個儀式。主要成份爲 Epstein-Barr 病毒。有別於大多數減毒病毒是爲了研發疫苗而設計的，這個病毒的培養動機來自於娛樂。

這個食譜兼病毒株是設計透過加入病毒來優化傳統清酒釀造的過程。

整個釀造過程爲期一週。第一天，煮兩杯米直到熟透後加入 Epstein-Barr 病毒。咀嚼一湯匙的米飯，接著吐到玻璃罐中。重複這個過程直到所有米飯都嚼過並且被唾液分解。

用紗布將罐口蓋住，在陰涼環境中放置五天。約一天後罐子內容物會開始發泡並散發些微酒精氣味。

第七天，邀請賓客來共同飲用釀好的酒。這酒將讓肌肉稍微刺痛，有些人則有較嚴重的身體疼痛。雖然聽起來很危險，但這個品系的 Epstein-Barr 病毒只會發作十二小時。在這段時間內，所有賓客邊享受微醺且微痛的體驗，邊一同咀嚼米飯釀造下一桶酒。

SM Brewery

Here is the very first viral drink using viral agents - although not typically a 'drink' as such.
This is a recipe, but also a ritual. The main ingredient is a weakened, controlled strain of Epstein-Barr Virus.
Unlike other attenuated viruses developed for vaccines, this is developed only for pleasure.
It was designed to improving the old traditional sake brewing process by including viral agents...

The whole brewing process takes about a week.
On the first day, cook two cups of rice until done.
Mix the Epstein-Barr Virus into the rice. Put one spoonful of rice in the mouth, chew the rice thoroughly, and then spit into a jar. Repeat this process until all the rice is chewed and broken down by the saliva.

Cover the jar with a cheese cloth. Let stand for at least 5 days in a dark, cool place.
The jar should start to bubble after a day with slightly alcoholic smell.

On the 7th day, invite your guests and drink the wine together. The wine will create a tingling sensation in muscles or sometitmes slightly more severe body aches. Although it might sound dangerous, this specific strain of Epstein-Barr Virus will only remain active for 12 hours. As all the guests are enjoying the tipsy-achy experience, more rice is provided for the guests to chew when drinking to brew the next batch of wine.

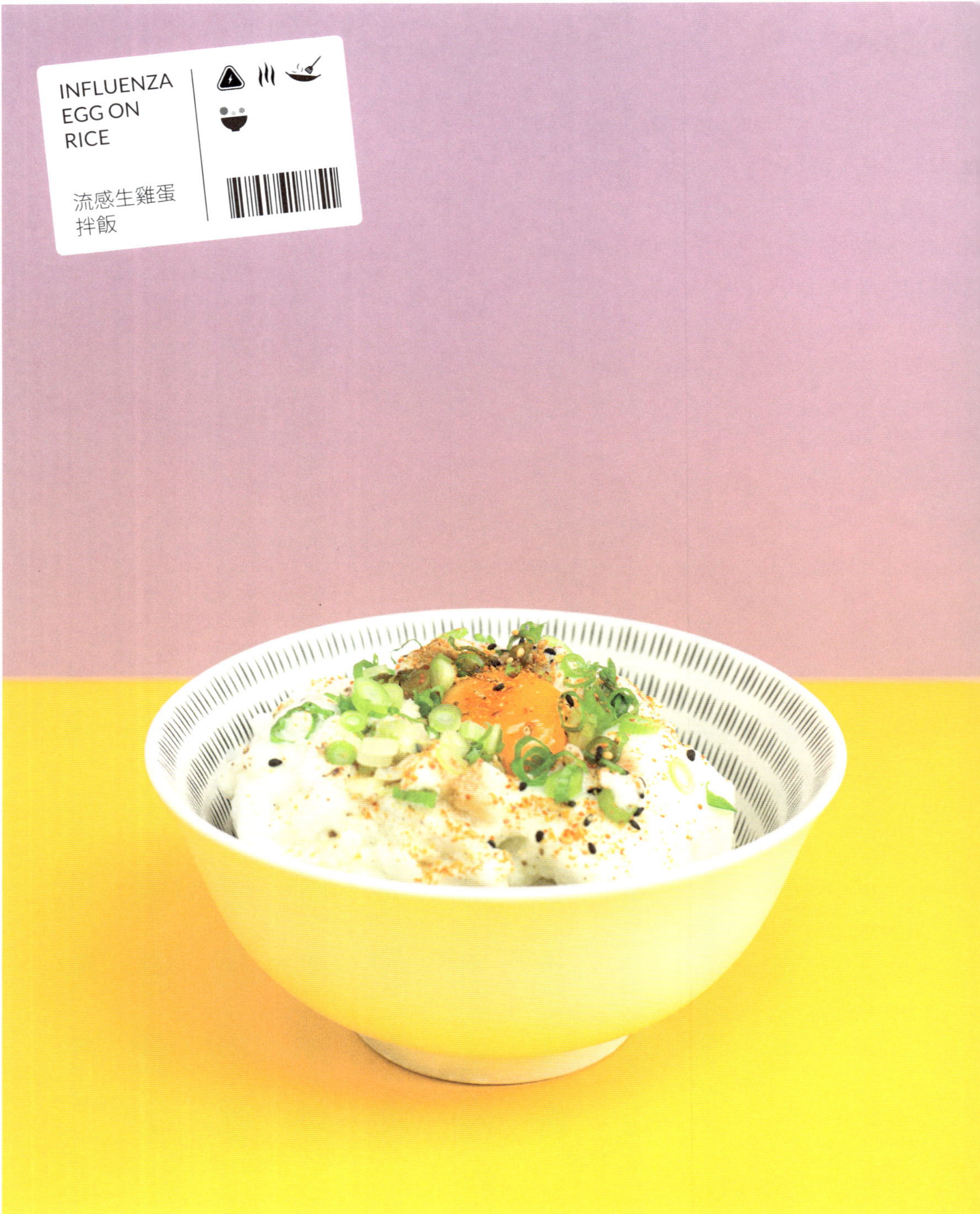
INFLUENZA EGG ON RICE
流感生雞蛋拌飯

流感生雞蛋拌飯

蒸飯，將蒸好的飯盛入碗中。

小心地將含有食品級流感病毒的雞蛋打開。這個流感雞蛋有時也被作爲季節流感疫苗使用，通常由疫苗生產公司製造，在藥房內販售。將雞蛋蛋白與蛋黃以乾淨的湯匙分開。

將蛋白放在乾淨並乾燥的金屬碗內，用攪拌器打發。

將打發蛋白放在蒸好的飯中央。

將生蛋黃放在打發蛋白上。

淋上醬油與香料調味。

這道菜會讓喉嚨產生刺刺麻麻的感覺，並佐以十二個小時的低燒。這道菜每年在新的流感疫苗生產出來後可以吃一次。

Influenza Egg on Rice

Prepare and steam the rice. Once done, scoop the hot steaming rice into a bowl.

Carefully open an egg containing food grade influenza virus which also known as a form of vaccine. It is usually distributed by vaccine production companies and can be bought from the pharmacy. Separate the egg white and the egg yolk using dry, clean utensil. Spoon is usually handy in this case.

Put the egg white in an extremely clean and dry metal bowl, use a beater to whip the egg white until it forms a sturdy foam.

Put the foam in the centre of the steamed rice.

Put the egg yolk on top.

Season with soy sauce and spice.

This dish will induce slight tingling sensation in the throat along with low fever that lasts for 12 hours. It can be experienced once every year when the new predicted strain of influenza vaccine is being produced.

Coliflower Mosaic Virus

First plant virus with its genome sequenced,
a common tool for GMO plants.

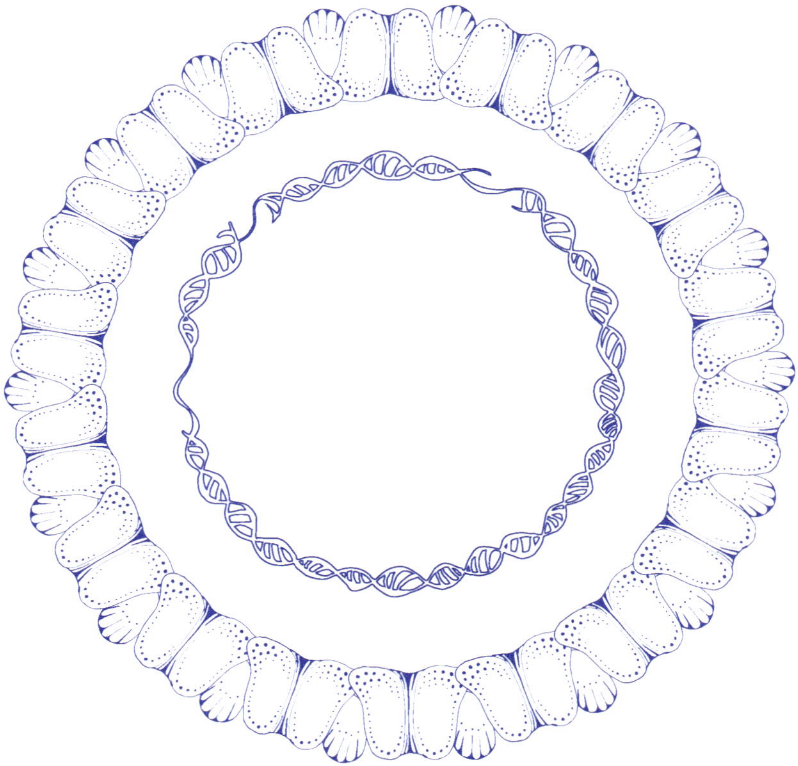

Chapter Four

Dynamic Cuisine

動態烹飪

ca. 2051

西元 2051 年前後

病毒可以作爲菌株群組來使用，而非單獨的病毒菌株。病毒「群組」的設計原則爲「將多物種集合視爲單一宿主、並將反應時間納入考量」。此烹飪原則就如同於在盤中指揮一首小型交響樂。

Viruses can be used as collections of strains instead of separate individual virus strains. The design of virus 'sets' is based on the principles of seeing a collection of different species as one 'host' and taking the duration of time into consideration. It is similar to orchestrating a mini symphony within a dish.

瞬變雞尾酒

自２０４０年代後期瞬變雞尾酒第一次出現後便極受歡迎，無論是商業或是自行釀造，有各式各樣不同的瞬變雞尾酒做法。

瞬變雞尾酒基本上分成兩部分：飲料本體與活化劑。這種飲料本體一定是某種細菌或酵母的發酵飲料，例如啤酒、紅酒、克菲爾、水克菲爾或紅茶菌。飲料本體中微生物組成越複雜，則該雞尾酒越變化多端。活化劑由多種病毒組成，可向食品級病毒供應商訂購。活化劑會對飲料本體中的微生物產生不同反應，例如殺死特定微生物，或讓不同的微生物在不同時間得到新的能力與效用。

最早出現的瞬變雞尾酒是種商業用雞尾酒。在紅茶菌風靡歐洲以後，開始有專門生產紅茶菌的生物科技公司開始發展一組稱爲「紅茶菌之友」的病毒組合。「紅茶菌之友」包含三種不同病毒：KomYeastA、KomBacA、KomYeastD。KomYeastA在短時間內加快酵母產生酒精的速度，使紅茶菌在十分鐘內變得像啤酒。KomYeastD 專門殺死酵母，酵母的死亡會賦予紅茶菌肉的氣味。最後，KomBacA 加快細菌生產乙酸的速度，讓肉味紅茶菌啤酒轉變爲紅茶菌醋。

紅茶菌與紅茶菌之友會盛裝在兩公升連水龍頭玻璃瓶中供飲用。紅茶菌之友在玻璃瓶裝著紅茶菌上桌的那個瞬間加入，並開始反應。當賓客開始飲用時，紅茶菌逐漸依序變成紅茶菌啤酒、肉味紅茶菌啤酒、最後成爲紅茶菌醋。飲用法爲使用裝了冰塊的杯子隨時承裝，冰鎮後飲用。

瞬變雞尾酒的概念後來被推廣到其他飲品上。隨著食品級病毒公司的蓬勃發展，這個技術開始被家庭私釀廣泛使用，一般人可以從這些公司訂購自己設計的病毒組合來使用。例如現在市面上特別受歡迎的就有變色啤酒、質感變化葡萄酒、黏度變化克菲爾等飲品。

Temporal Cocktail

Temporal cocktail has become extremely popular since its first appearance in the late 2040s. There is a huge variety of temporal cocktail recipes available, both commercially and for DIY home brewing.

Temporal cocktails basically consist of two parts: the drink, and the activator. The drink is always a bacterial / yeast fermented drink: beer, wine, kefir, water kefir, or kombucha. The more sophisticated the microbes' composition is, the more fascinating the drink becomes. The activator is a group of viruses, which can usually be ordered from a food-grade virus supplier. They react to different microbes in the drink, either killing the microbes or providing them with new abilities throughout time.The very first temporal cocktail was a commercial one. After the kombucha hype in Europe, a biotech company originally mass producing kombucha designed a set of viruses called 'kombucha mate'.

Kombucha mate consists of three different viruses: KomYeastA, KomBacA, and KomYeastD. KomYeastA accelerates the alcohol production speed of yeast in a very short period of time, making the kombucha beer-like within 10 minutes. KomYeastD targets the yeast in kombucha, giving the kombucha a meaty taste. Subsequently, KomBacA accelerates the production of acetic acid in bacteria. The meaty alcoholic kombucha then turns into a 'kombucha vinegar'.

The kombucha + kombucha mate is served in a 2 litre jar with a tap. Kombucha mate will be added to kombucha as soon as the jar is brought to the table. As people drink, the taste changes from kombucha to beer-like kombucha, meaty beer, and then vinegar kombucha. Guests can pour the kombucha from the tap into their own cup filled with ice to enjoy.

Later, the temporal cocktail idea was extended to other drinks. As food-grade virus companies flourish, the technology has become easily accessible for home-brewing. Ordinary individuals can order their own self-designed virus collection from various companies. Nowadays there are colour-changing beers, texture changing wines and viscosity changing kefir just to name a few. They are all extremely popular on the market.

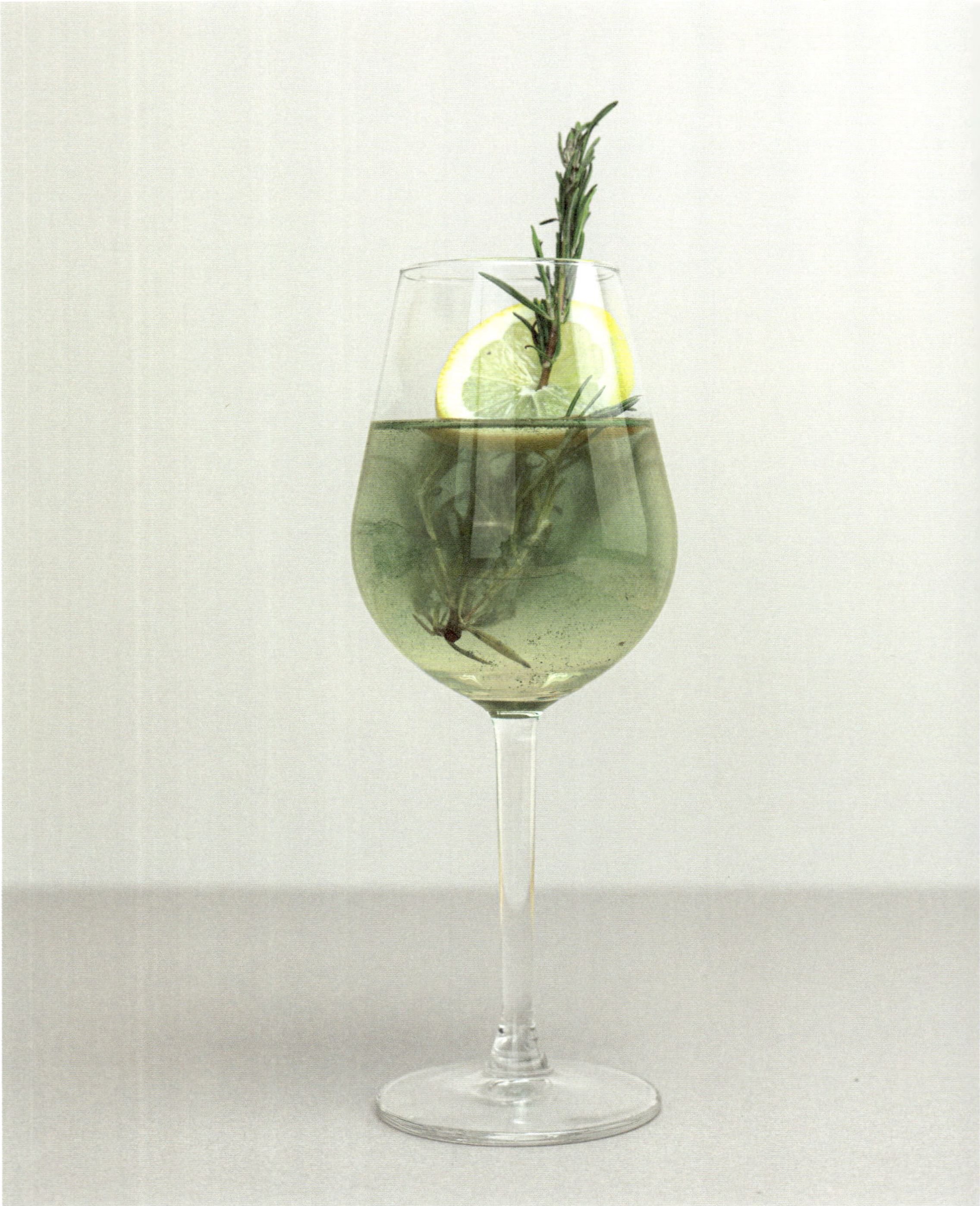

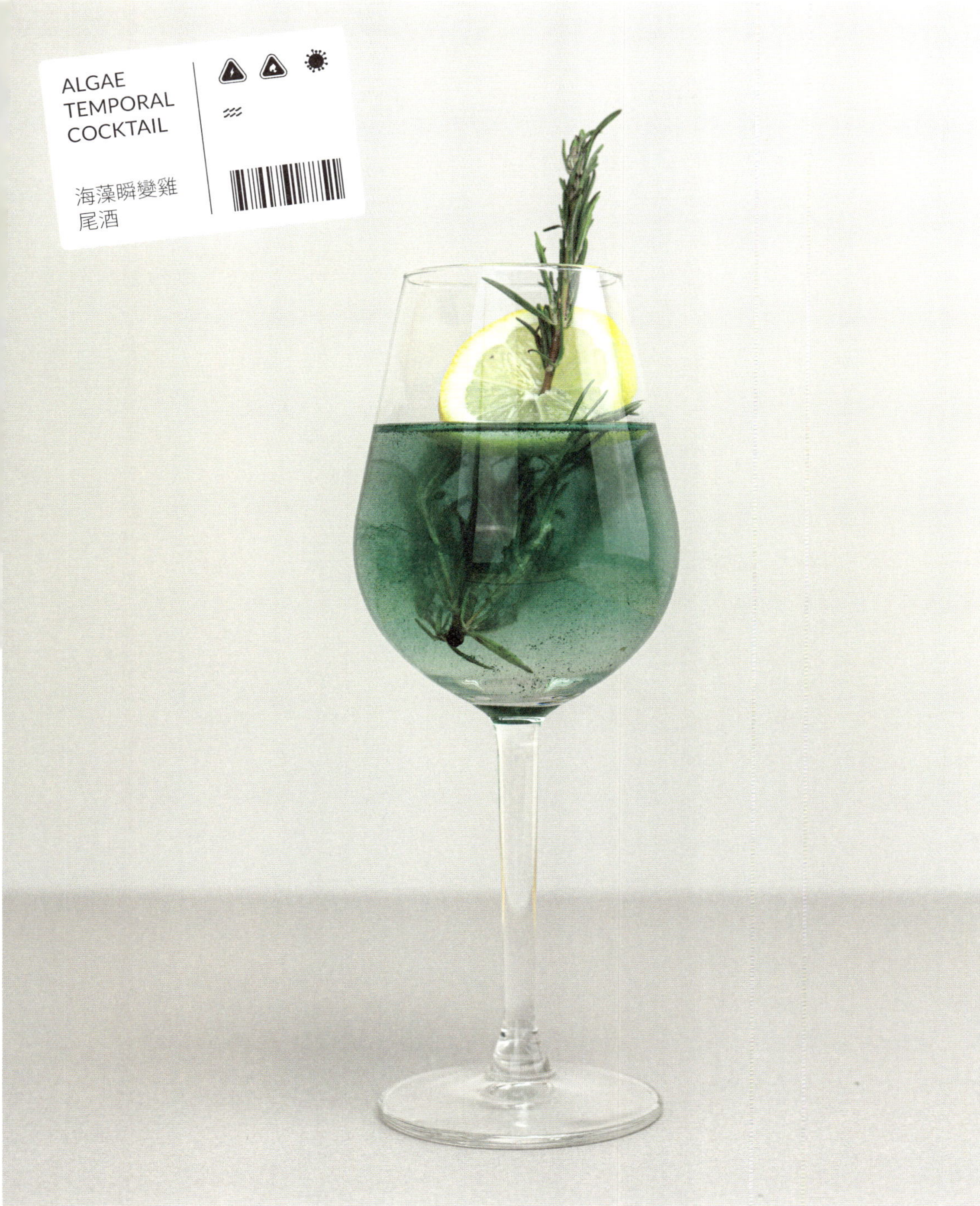
ALGAE
TEMPORAL
COCKTAIL
海藻瞬變雞
尾酒

酸甜老麵

這個食譜源自於古老的酸麵包發酵技術，並經由病毒技術改造。酸麵包發酵是經由乳酸菌和酵母菌組合的複雜微生物菌群共同發酵而成，這些菌群的採集方式爲以果汁開始發酵，並定期每十二個小時餵養麵粉與水，持續一週。這個過程會讓乳酸菌與酵母菌成爲麵粉中的優勢族群，而形成酸麵糰。由於採集到的野生菌群各家不同，因此產生的酸麵包氣味也各家不同，其複雜而多層次的味道廣受人喜愛。

酸甜老麵是病毒版的酸麵糰，經由加入病毒於酸麵包的微生物菌群中，並增加發酵的步驟，可以產生之前單由乳酸菌與酵母菌發酵所無法散發的味道。

酸甜麵糰母可以從食品級病毒公司購買。這個麵糰母包含兩種病毒，在不同環境下會在菌群中佔主導地位。第一種病毒爲 SouDPhoto，帶有光合作用基因，會感染乳酸菌並讓乳酸菌獲得有氧光合作用，將二氧化碳與水合成爲醣。這個新增加的能力讓酸甜麵糰可以在氣密的環境中進行正常的日夜循環，就像生態瓶一樣。白天，酸甜麵糰透過光合作用產生氧氣與醣，夜晚使用白天產生的氧氣進行發酵。這讓酸麵糰變得比較甜、並且可以維持更久。

第二種病毒爲 SouDCillus，在麵糰中的酵母菌產生酒精時開始反應，將酒精合成爲纖維，讓麵糰產生特殊的質感。

如此發酵的酸甜麵糰最常被使用於筋道麵點，其口感介於麵包與麻糬之間。

Sour-Sweet-Dough

This recipe originates from the old sourdough fermentation method with a viral extension. Sourdough is fermented by a microbial community consisting of lactobacilli and yeast. The microbes are harvested from the wild by growing a flour culture with a juice starter and adding flour and water every 12 hours, every day, for a week. This allows the wild lactobacilli and yeast to become dominant in this flour-based 'sourdough starter'. Sourdough tastes very different from one to another due to different microbial communities during cultivation. The sophisticated taste of sourdough is loved by many.

Sour-sweet-dough is the viral version of sourdough. By adding viruses to the microbial community of the sourdough and by adding more stages to the fermentation, tastes that were previously impossible to generate by with only the microbiome itself can be created.

The sour-sweet-dough starter can be ordered from companies that produce food-grade viruses. The starter contains two different viruses which become dominant under different environmental conditions. The first virus is SouDPhoto, which carries a gene for photosynthesis. It infects the lactobacilli and gives lactobacilli the ability to perform oxygenic photosynthesis, which combines CO2 with water to make sugar. It allows the sourdough starter to be fermented in an air-tight container with normal day-night cycles. In the day time the sourdough starter goes through photosynthesis generating oxygen and sugar, and during the night the sourdough starter uses the oxygen produced in the day time to conduct fermentation. This makes the sourdough sweeter and it lasts longer.

The second virus, SouDCillus, becomes active when the yeast in the dough starts to create alcohol. It converts the alcohol into cellulose, forming interesting textures in the dough.

The sour-sweet-dough is used most often for bouncy pastry with a texture somewhere between bread and mochi.

Enterobacteria Phage T4

Easy to grow in *E. coli*, used as a model for molecular evolution with the potential usage for delivering nanoparticles to the targeted tissues.

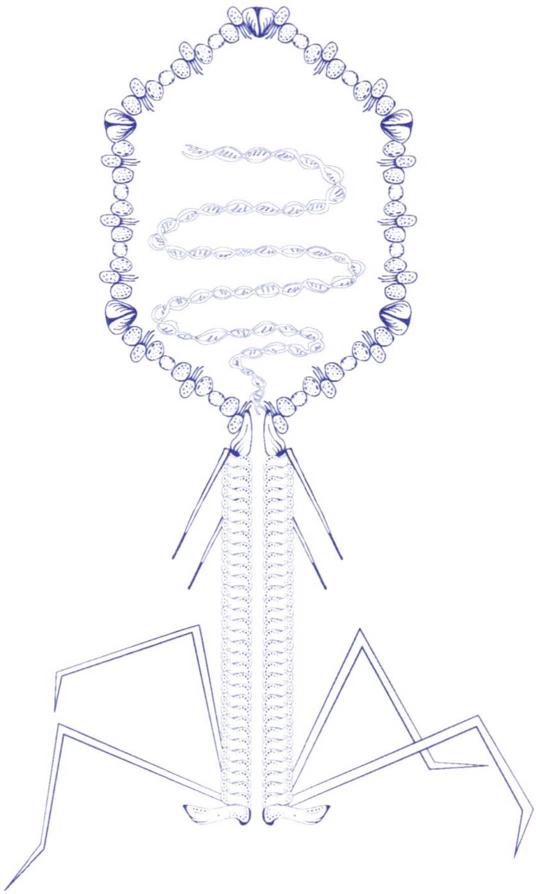

Chapter Five

Ecosystem Cuisine

生態美食

ca. 2065

西元 2065 年前後

生態美食旨在讓生態系中每一個份子都能享受到這道餐點。不論微生物、動物、人類、或介於有生命與無生命之間的病毒，所有具有消化與複製的能力的個體皆爲客人。

生態美食的座右銘爲「所有人皆涵括在內，一個都不少」。生態美食廚師的最高目標爲讓生態系中的所有客人都同樣滿意與愉悅。在生態系中誰被吃了、有多少個體被吃了，取決於每個個體對於「存活」的定義。

「平衡」是終極原則，只有當生與死平衡時，這道菜才是被享受的。設計菜餚時，「吃」與「食物」的定義需要被審慎檢視並重新定義。

Ecosystem cuisine is created for the whole ecosystem to enjoy. All agents which possess the ability to digest and replicate are guests, whether they are microbes, animals, humans, or even semi-living viruses. The motto of ecosystem cuisine is 'no one gets left behind, everyone is included'. The highest goal of an ecosystem cuisine chef is to have all parties within the system satisfied and entertained.

Who gets eaten and how many of them get eaten would depend on the definition of 'survival' of each individual.

Balance is the ultimate guideline.
Only when death / survival is well-balanced will there be an enjoyment of food. The definitions of 'eating' and 'food' have to be carefully considered each time.

生態系零和早餐

這個早餐在日出時刻於種滿香菜與蔬菜，有肥沃黑土的後院中進行。玻璃瓶中裝著雨水與可以同時感染植物與人類唾腺的病毒，讓參加者每人拿著一瓶雨水溫柔的灌溉泥土。當雨水碰到土壤，土壤中的放線菌釋出孢子，讓空氣中充滿了下雨的味道。參加者輕撫香草們，讓羅勒與番茄的氣味與雨水混合。花園中前一晚被眞菌病毒雨水澆過的土地已長出蘑菇。這些蘑菇從水觸發菌絲體開始形成子實體，當子實體吸收著土壤中的養分，眞菌病毒將藍色生物螢光基因鑲嵌進蘑菇基因中，讓蘑菇發著淡淡的藍光在夜裡長大。

太陽升起的過程中，將木頭劈成適當大小，支起烤肉架，堆好火種與木塊，生火。直至木頭燃燒到出現灰色，烤肉可以開始了。這個過程約需二十分鐘。收成蘑菇、番茄與其他香草。因爲剛日出，天尚暗，採集時仍能看到蘑菇在黑暗中發出微光。

將蔬菜們串在長叉上，置於烤肉架上燒烤。當蔬菜們開始焦黑變皺，撒上香料。

人類參與者邊吃蔬菜，蔬菜中還存活著的病毒邊開始在他們的唾液腺中感染、生長，並再透過唾液傳播回長叉上。病毒在唾液腺中繁殖的同時也讓唾液腺產生特殊的蛋白質，跟著病毒一起散播出細胞外，產生複雜的味道。

長叉在食用完畢後，以植物支撐架的角色被重複利用，繼續存在於花園中，並進一步帶著病毒感染花園中的植物。烤肉後的灰燼一部分變成堆肥，另一部分拿去將稻草消毒後作爲菌絲體培養的介質。

Ecosystem Zero Breakfast

The breakfast is served in a backyard with rich black soil and plenty of herbs and vegetables, right at the moment the sun dawns. Rainwater containing viruses, which live both in plants and human saliva glands, is served in jars. Each of the human guests takes a jar of rainwater and slowly pours the rainwater into the soil. The Smell of rain rises from the soil as the Actinomycetes bacteria release their spores. Human guests then touch the herbs softly with their hands. As the hands move through the plants, the smell of basil and tomato mix with the smell of rain. The part of the garden treated the previous night with rainwater mixed with mycoviruses already has mushrooms growing.

The water initiates a series of reactions in the soil, activating the mycelium and triggering the forming of fruiting bodies. As the fruiting bodies absorb the nutrients in the soil, the mycoviruses containing blue bioluminescence genes enter the mushrooms. The mushrooms sprout during the night, shining dim blue.

As the sun rises, chop the wood into medium pieces. Roll out the charcoal grill. Stack up the fire starter with wood chips, and light it up. Let the wood burn until it starts to turn grey. Now it is ready for barbecue. It will take about 20 mins to heat up. Harvest the mushrooms, tomatoes and other desired herbs. Because the sun has just dawned, it is still comparatively dark. The mushrooms are still shining with a blueish tint.

Thread the vegetables onto the skewers, and barbecue on the grill. As the vegetables start to brown and their skins become wrinkled, sprinkle the herbs onto the vegetables.

As human guests feast on the grilled vegetables, the plant viruses in the raw part of the vegetables find their habitat in human saliva glands. The viruses enter the glands and replicate. As humans eat the vegetables from the skewers, the replicated viruses also attach themselves onto the skewers. As the viruses replicate, they also trick the saliva glands into producing protein molecules that are released along with viruses, creating a very sophisticated taste.

The skewers are then reused back in the garden as supporting structures for the plants, further infecting the plants in the garden. The wood ashes are used as soil fertilisers, while some other ashes are used to pasteurise the straws for mycelium cultivation.

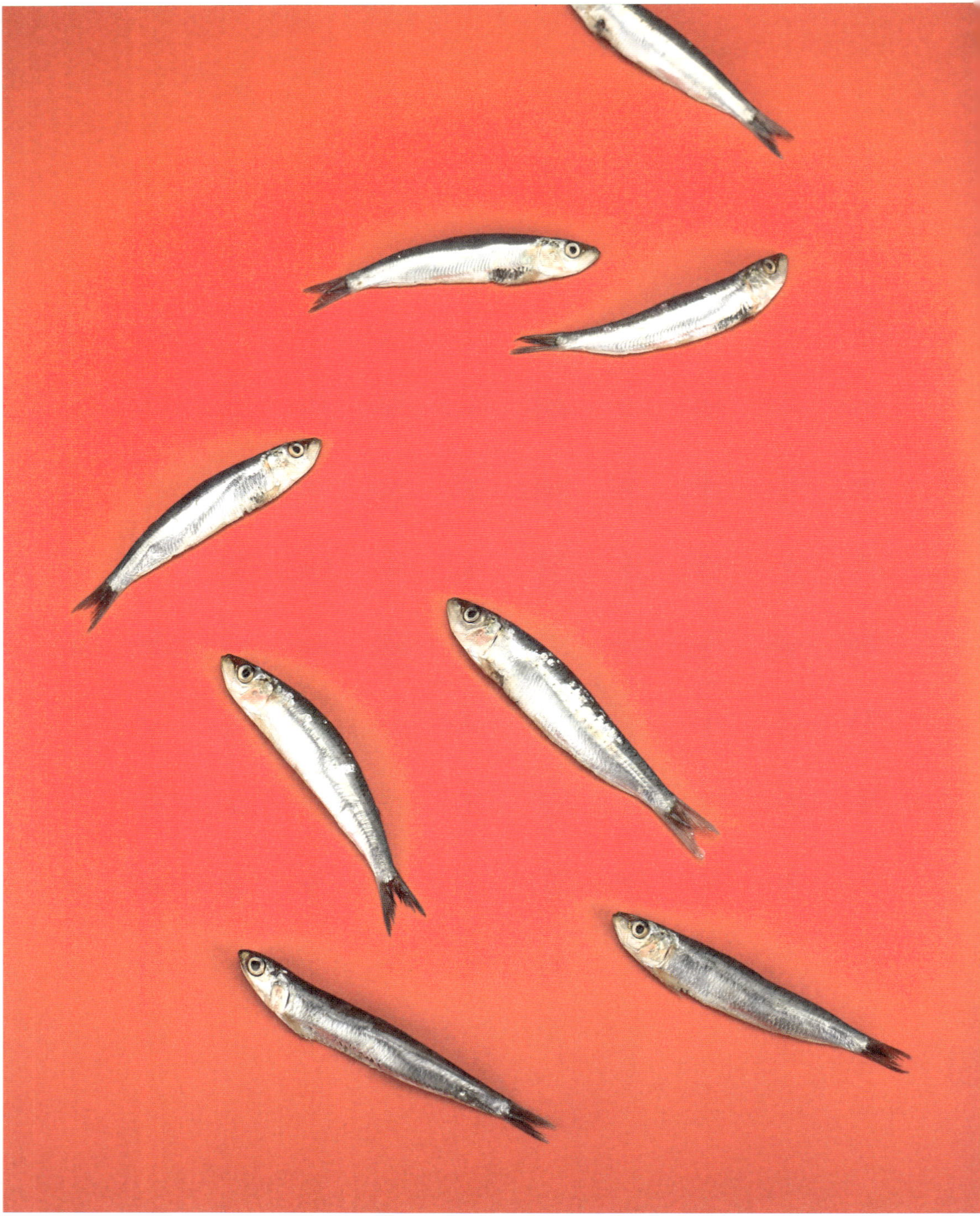

離岸晚午餐

人類賓客在岸邊集合後乘遊艇航向離岸藻華，多艘小船在那等候著。抵達後，人類賓客們搭上小船自由的在藻華中划行。每艘小船搭載著一位廚師兼漁夫。手持一瓶搭配好的海生病毒，人類賓客們將病毒倒入海洋中，啟動整個宴會。

病毒們是這個宴會中的第一群嘉賓。經由感染浮游生物與海洋細菌，病毒在牠們體內複製後將他們的細胞溶解，並釋放出溶解有機質（DOM dissolved organic matters）至水中。這些分子是邀請浩闊海洋中其他生物如魚蝦、水鳥等生物一同參加這次宴會的邀請函。

隨著溶解有機質被風與浪帶到各種動物的鼻腔中，就彷彿是在海洋中響起了開飯鐘聲。沙丁魚最先到來，以海面之下成群旋風般的旋轉而至，獵捕正在忙著自殺以阻止細菌複製的浮游生物。病毒複製就像是連鎖反應般，每隻被病毒感染並在體內複製後炸開的浮游生物都會釋放出千萬隻病毒，繼續感染更多浮游生物。當病毒忙著繁衍複製，開心的沙丁魚也在他們之間大口吞噬著一團團的浮游生物。

漁夫趁著水下沙丁魚群環繞在船四週開始放網，網沉至魚群深處補起滿滿的沙丁魚。這些魚需清理後醃漬或是用平底鍋煎至金黃，撒上鹽與胡椒，佐香草上桌。

當沙丁魚正在吃與被吃的同時，其他賓客從小型魚到大型魚逐漸到達。海豚、海豹、鯊魚、旗魚、魟魚，根據這個宴會的地理位置會有不同的參與者。鳥類，特別是海鳥，也聞香而來。隨著牠們的到來，宴會來到最高潮。

這時，藻類開始「發酵」，讓拍打小船的海浪打出泡沫。最後，以人類能感知到的濃度，豐富的蛋白質氣味從海中升起，這是海藻死亡的訊號，也是我們說的「海的味道」。這個氣味更爲用餐的人們觀看海中發生的事增添氣氛。

海面下二十公尺處，大型動物開始他們的狩獵之舞。海豚、海豹與鮪魚穿梭在沙丁魚群中獵捕，促使沙丁魚群不斷地變換形狀。海鳥子彈般衝刺進水中咬得滿嘴魚。鯨魚有時最後抵達，一次張大嘴吞下一整群的沙丁魚。狡猾如常的人類賓客抓緊機會同時獵捕大型魚，鮪魚就是目標之一。而當人類賓客用餐完畢，剩餘的殘渣則餵回給海鳥。

在四個小時的大快朵頤與消化之後，人類賓客半裸著跳進海中，將自己的一部分貢獻給海中細菌，讓海洋細菌在皮膚上用餐。有些時候，更豪放的人會再多貢獻一些含氮液體給微生物們。

Late Lunch Offshore

Human guests are gathered and sailing off the coast on a yacht towards an algae bloom offshore where boats await. Upon arrival, human guests embark from the smaller boats that roll freely within the blooming area. Each boat has a crew member who is at the same time a fisherman and a cook. Carrying bottles of marine viruses in hand, the human guests pour the viruses into the ocean which onsets the whole banquet.

The viruses would be the first to enjoy the meal. By infecting the planktons and marine bacteria, the viruses first replicate within the planktons and bacteria. Later lysis opens these hosts, releasing tiny molecules of DOM (dissolved organic matter into the water. These molecules are the invitation sent out to other organisms like fish, shrimps, and birds, across the deep, wide ocean.

As the DOM travel through waves and wind and enter the nostrils of different animals, it is like a bell announcing the presence of an abundant meal. First come the sardines. The sardines arrive in a shoal, constantly rotating like a tornado underneath the water. The sardines hunt the floating planktons while the planktons are busy killing themselves to interrupt virus replications. Virus replication is a chain reaction, each burst plankton releases millions of viruses which infect more plankton. While viruses are occupied with propagation, the happy sardines also come along and swallow lumps of planktons at a time.

Surrounded by the underwater shoals of sardines, the fisherman-cook starts to release funnel fishnets deep within the shoals and catches a handful of sardines. The fished sardines are cleaned and either marinated or lightly fried using a pan with a pinch of salt and pepper, and are served with herbs to the human guests.

While the sardines are eating and being eaten, other guests arrive. First the small fishes then the larger ones. Dolphins, seals, sharks, sailfish, devil rays... It all depends on the geographical location where the banquet is being held, the attendance varies. Birds, particularly sea birds, also join. As they arrive, the banquet welcomes its highest point.

Meanwhile, the algae start to 'ferment'. Foams appears with each sea wave hitting the boat. Finally, with a dosage perceivable to the human, the scent of rich protein rises from the ocean. It is the sign of algae death —what we called 'the smell of the ocean'. This aroma adds to the atmosphere for diners on the boat while being witness to what is happening underneath.

20 meters down under, the larger animals start their hunting dance. Dolphins, seals, and tuna glide in and out of the sardine shoal while eating, causing the shoal to change shape. Sea birds shoot into the water like bullets and grab a mouth full of fish. Whales sometimes come last, swim towards the family of sardines with their mouths wide open, sieving through the water and swallowing a lump of fish. Human guests, as cunning as they always are, fish the other larger animals as well, tuna being one of them. As the human guests finish eating, the leftovers are fed to the birds.

At last, after 4 hours of feasting and digesting, the human guests jump into the ocean half naked, contributing a part of themselves for the ocean bacteria — for the bacteria dine on their skin. And sometimes, the daring ones will also gift the microbes a bit of watery nitrogen source.

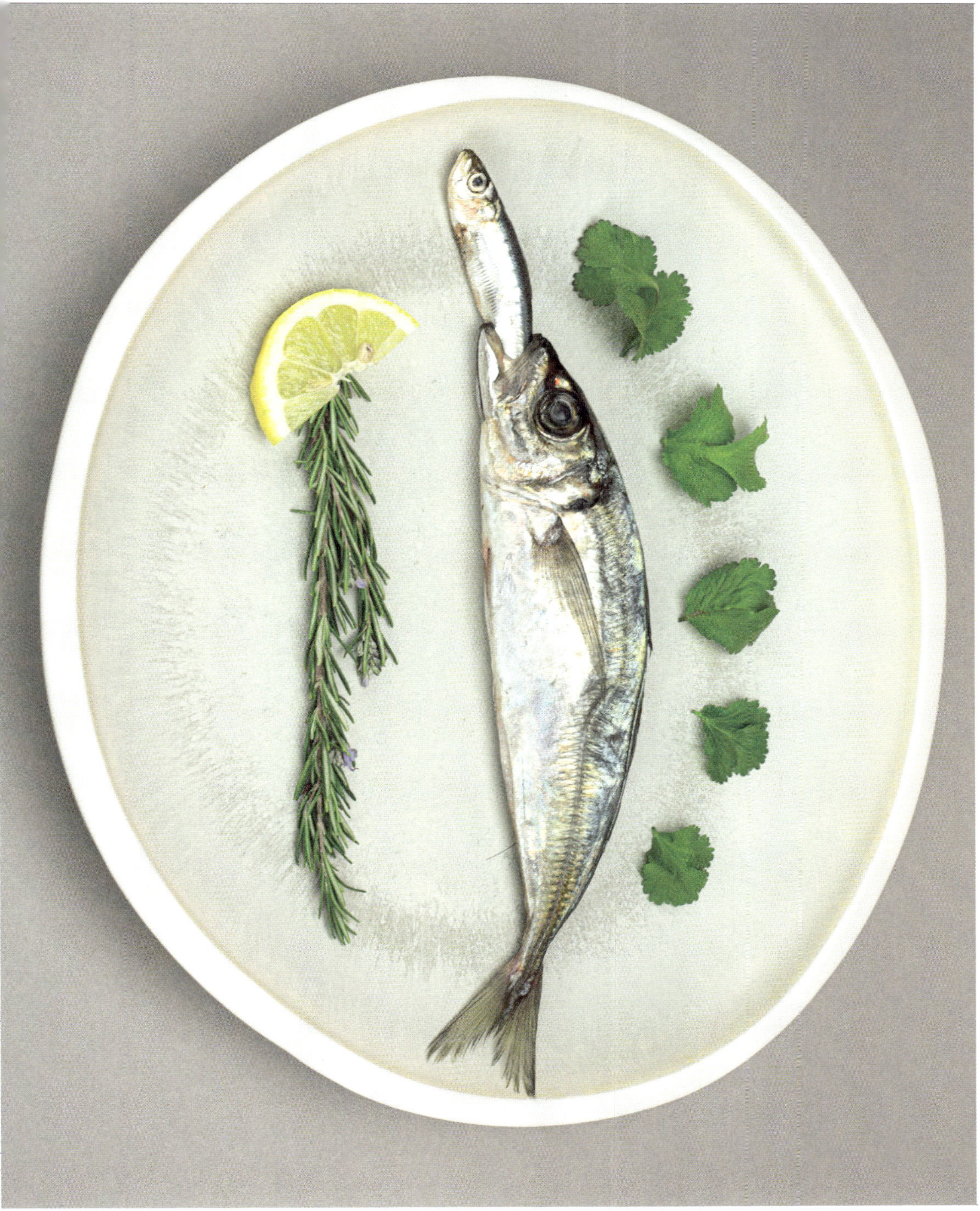

Set Margins' #5

Title: Virophilia
Title: 病毒之愛
Subtitle: The 2070 revised edition of the Postnatural Cookbook
Chinese Subtitle: 2070年後自然再版病毒食譜書
Original Subtitle: Cookbook for 22nd-Century Virophilists
Original Chinese Subtitle: 給二十二世紀病毒愛好者的食譜書

Author: Pei-Ying Lin
Editor: Pei-Ying Lin

Scientific Inspiration comes from the conversations with Miranda de Graaf, Rene van der Vlugt, and Corina Brussaard.

Any references to historical events, real people, or real places are used fictitiously.

Names, characters, and places are products of the author's imagination.

Graphic designers: Lisa Ladent & Aurélie Morra

Fonts: Lato by Łukasz Dziedzic ©tyPoland
Coconat by Sara Lavazza ©Colllectttivo
金萱鮮摘 半糖 ©JustFont
源樣明體 © But Ko based on Source Han Serif

Editorial advisor: Freek Lomme

Proofreader: Alexandra Fraser, Chia-Wei Hsu, Yu-Ting Cheng

Image editor: Pei-Ying Lin

Printer: Printon, Tallinn (EST)

Made possible thanks to the generous support of AirWG, Waag Society, Mediamatic, 3PackageDeal, Amsterdam Fonds voor de Kunst, Vrije Universiteit Amsterdam, Stichting Cultuur Eindhoven.

Pei-Ying Lin would like to thank Toby Kiers, Miranda de Graaf, Rene van der Vlugt, Corina Brussaard, Jos Looije, Ishtar Hsu, Cecile Espinasse, Min-Shu Huang, Yu-Ting Cheng, Guo-Ling Tsai, Yen-An Chen, Li-Ting Chen, Angela Ying-Jung Chen, Dymfy van Meel, Yun Wah Lam and all the participants for their advice and feedback.

Special thanks to the Culinary Virus Research Lab, Viral Cuisines Museum, and VaccineBeauty Co. for their share of knowledge and history.

Set Margins'
www.setmargins.press